handy homework helper

English

Writer:
Lynne Blanton, Ph.D.

Consultant:
Dorothy F. King, Ed.D.

Publications International, Ltd.

Louis Weber, C.E.O.
Publications International, Ltd.
7373 North Cicero Avenue
Lincolnwood, Illinois 60646

Manufactured in China.

8 7 6 5 4 3 2 1

ISBN: 0-7853-1953-0

Lynne Blanton, Ph.D., is a writer and editor with Creative Services, Inc., a publisher of educational materials for over 15 years. She has served as editor for both Rand McNally and Riverside Publishing Company and has a B.A. in English and History from Birmingham-Southern College and a Ph.D. in Communications from the University of Illinois.

Dorothy F. King is an Associate Professor of Early Childhood Education at the University of New Mexico-Gallup and has served as Chair for the National Council of Teachers of English Commission on Curriculum. She also is a consultant with Research and Training Associates, Inc., for whom she provides technical assistance services for the Office of Indian Education Programs.

Cover photography: Siede Preis Photography

Models and agencies: McBlaine & Associates, Inc.: Kristy Evans; **Royal Modeling Management:** Trevor Hocken, Sara McHale, Mark Elliot Thostesen.

Illustrations: Chris Reed

Contents

About This Book

Homework takes time and a lot of hard work. Many students would say it's their least favorite part of the school day. But it's also one of the most important parts of your school career because it does so much to help you learn. Learning gives you knowledge, and knowledge gives you power.

Homework gives you a chance to review the material you've been studying so you understand it better. It lets you work on your own, which can give you confidence and independence. Doing school work at home also gives your parents a way to find out what you're studying in school.

Everyone has trouble with their homework from time to time, and *Handy Homework Helper: English* can help you when you run into a problem. This book was prepared with the help of educational specialists. It offers quick, simple explanations of the basic material that you're studying in school. If you get stuck on an idea or have trouble finding some information, *Handy Homework Helper: English* can help clear it up for you. It can also help your parents help you by giving them a fast refresher course in the subject.

This book is clearly organized by the topics you'll be studying in English. A quick look at the Table of Contents will tell you which chapter covers the area you're working on. You can probably guess which chapter includes what you need and then flip through the chapter until you find it. For even more help finding what you're looking for, look up key words related to what you're studying in the Index. You might find material faster that way, and you might also find useful information in a place you wouldn't have thought to look.

Remember that different teachers and different schools take different approaches to teaching English. For that reason, we recommend that you talk with your teacher about using this homework guide. You might even let your teacher look through the book so he or she can help you use it in a way that best matches what you're studying at school.

English and You

You are already an accomplished user of the English language. After all, you speak and write English all the time, and people understand you. But sometimes you may need to know more about the language or be reminded of what you already know. This book contains information on grammar, mechanics, and writing that you can use whenever you think you need it. It's a reference tool that can help you when you are completing assignments for English or any other topic that requires writing.

The dialect used in the *English Homework Guide* is Standard English. A dialect is a specific version of a language. People who speak different dialects of a language understand each other, but they might use different words for some things. There are many different dialects in English. Everyone uses a dialect, and no dialect is "bad." But Standard English has one major advantage: It is the dialect used by people with political, economic, and social power. By learning Standard English, you increase your own possiblilities for success in our society.

This book has three parts: Grammar, Mechanics, and Writing. "Grammar" covers sentences and parts of speech—the basic building blocks of the English language. "Mechanics" explains the rules governing capitalization and punctuation in English. "Writing" explains the stages of the writing process and discusses skills related to writing, such as using a dictionary or a thesaurus and remembering how to spell words.

Like a dictionary, thesaurus, or any other reference source, the *English Homework Guide* is meant to be one of many tools available to you—a tool that you decide when and how to use.

Grammar

The main point of language is to communicate meaning. A person is judged by the skill with which he or she communicates meaning in speech or writing. Grammar *ADJECTIVE* is one tool for getting your meaning across. Grammar describes the way the English language works.

Adverb You already know a lot about English grammar. With practice, using the grammar of Standard English will become a habit, something you do not even think about. And when you use grammar correctly, you communicate your thoughts clearly.

Usually, we listen to what people say, not how they say it. But if they do not use language and grammar well, we may be distracted from the what by the how. To make sure people pay attention to what you are saying (or writing), you *Verb* must use grammar and your other language tools to communicate clearly.

This section explains everything from sentences to parts of speech. You will find plenty of examples to give you a feeling for how to use these constructions or words in your own writing. Learning to identify parts of speech is *Noun* important, but even more important is learning to use them to improve your writing. For example, you can use nouns to make your writing more precise, adjectives to make it more vivid, and pronouns to avoid repeating yourself. Learning to use parts of speech correctly will also help you avoid confusing and distracting your readers. Remember, you want them to concentrate on *what* you are saying, not *how* you are saying it.

Preposition

Sentences

What Is a Sentence?

A **sentence** is a group of words that expresses a complete thought or idea.

> The band has a rehearsal at 1:00.

This group of words is a sentence. It expresses a complete thought.

Is this group of words a sentence?

> The children in the band

The group of words tells about children in a band. But the words do not tell what the children are doing or what happens to them. The group of words does not express a complete thought, so it is not a sentence.

> Practiced all afternoon

This group of words tells about something that happened. But the words do not tell who or what practiced all afternoon. The group of words does not express a complete thought, so it is not a sentence.

A sentence tells what or whom the sentence is about. A sentence tells about something that happens.

> The children in the band practiced all afternoon.

A sentence can be very long or very short. A group of words that is not a sentence can be very long.

> Jane called.

> Running through the field and feeling the warm sun

Even though it is short, the first example is a sentence, because it expresses a complete thought. Even though it is long, the second example is not a sentence, because it does not express a complete thought.

Subjects and Predicates

A sentence has two parts: a subject and a predicate.

The **subject** of a sentence tells who or what the sentence is about.

> **Clarice's dog, Randall,** is a small, gray terrier.

> **The dogs in the neighborhood** began to bark.

The **predicate** of a sentence tells what the subject is or what the subject does.

> Clarice's dog, Randall, **is a small, gray terrier.**

> All the dogs in the neighborhood **began to bark.**

Every sentence can be divided into a subject and a predicate, and every word in a sentence is part of either the subject or the predicate.

Subject	Predicate
Thomas	gets up from the dinner table.
He	takes the dishes to the sink.
His dad	usually washes the dishes.
It	is Thomas's turn tonight.
Washing dishes	is not his favorite chore.
His sister Marie	offers to help him.

Usually, the subject is at or near the beginning of a sentence, and the predicate is at the middle or near the end of a sentence. But this may not be true in some sentences. Always ask the questions "Who or what is the sentence about?" and "What is the subject, or what is the subject doing?" to identify the subject and predicate of a sentence.

See page 15 for information on subjects in different locations in sentences.

Sentence Fragments and Run-on Sentences

Both sentence fragments and run-on sentences are confusing to readers. Sentence fragments are confusing because they leave out important information. Run-on sentences are confusing because they connect thoughts that should not be connected.

Sentence Fragments

A **sentence fragment** is a group of words that does not express a complete thought. It is only a part, or a *fragment*, of a sentence.

A fragment may have a subject but no predicate. It may have a predicate but no subject.

> During the storm, the tree in the yard.

> Covered the floor and everything on it.

To correct a sentence fragment, add whichever part is missing and make the fragment into a complete sentence.

> During the storm, the tree in the yard blew over and landed on the house.

> In the basement, mud and water covered the floor and everything on it.

Run-on Sentences

Two or more sentences written as though they were one sentence are called a **run-on sentence**. One sentence "runs on" into the next sentence.

There may be no end punctuation mark separating the first sentence from the second. A comma may be used incorrectly to separate the first sentence from the second.

> The rain poured down four inches fell in an hour.

> The rain poured down, four inches fell in an hour.

To correct a run-on sentence, add an end punctuation mark at the end of the first sentence. Capitalize the first word of the second sentence.

> The rain poured down. Four inches fell in an hour.

Simple Subjects and Predicates

Remember, a sentence can be divided into two parts: the subject and the predicate.

Subject   **Predicate**
The small, gray cat   ran under the bed.

The subject part of the example sentence is the **complete subject.** The complete subject is all the words that tell who or what the sentence is about. *The small, gray cat* is the complete subject of the example sentence.

The predicate part of the example sentence is the **complete predicate.** The complete predicate is all the words that tell what the subject is or what the subject does. *Ran under the bed* is the complete predicate of the example sentence.

Simple Subjects

The **simple subject** is the principal or most important word in the complete subject.

Look at these sentences:

Complete Subject   **Complete Predicate**
The small, gray cat   ran under the bed.
The door of the house   shut with a bang.
A girl with dark hair   stood at the window.

The most important word in the complete subject in the first sentence is *cat.* In the second sentence it's *door* and in the third sentence it's *girl.* These are the simple subjects.

To find the simple subject of a sentence, first find the predicate and then add *who* or *what.* Who ran under the bed? (cat) What shut with a bang? (door) Who stood at the window? (girl) The answer tells the simple subject.

Simple Predicates

The **simple predicate,** also called the **verb**, is the most important word in the complete predicate.

Look at these sentences:

Complete Subject	**Complete Predicate**
The big, black dog	howled at the moon.
One lone owl	sat in a tree.

The most important word in the complete predicate in the first sentence is *howled.* In the second sentence it's *sat.* These are the simple predicates, or verbs.

There are two kinds of verbs: action and state-of-being (or linking).

Action verbs express, or tell about, an action.

> Calvin **jumped** into the pool.
> He **swam** from one end to the other.

State-of-being verbs, which are also called **linking verbs,** express a state or condition. They link the subject to words that describe or identify it.

> The water in the pool **is** cool and blue.
> The afternoon sun **feels** warm.

The most common linking verb is the verb *be* in all its forms: *am, is, are, was, were, be, been, being.*

Other Common Linking Verbs

appear	get	remain
sound	become	grow
seem	stay	feel
look	smell	taste

Some linking verbs can also be also action verbs. *Smell* is an action verb in a sentence such as *Marika smells the flowers.*

See page 23 for information on action and linking verbs.

Compound Subjects and Predicates

The word *compound* comes from two Latin words meaning "to put together." A compound word is made by putting two or more smaller words together. So what would a compound subject or a compound predicate be?

Compound Subjects

A **compound subject** is made up of two or more subjects.

Subject	Predicate
Joanna and **Paul**	like to play board games.
Chess and **checkers**	are two of their favorites.

Both example sentences have compound subjects. That is, they each have two subjects: *Joanna* and *Paul, Chess* and *checkers.* The two subjects are joined by the conjunction *and.* A **conjunction** is a word that joins words or groups of words. Compound subjects may also be joined by the conjunction *or.*

Look at these sentences:

    Joanna, **Paul**, and **Maria** belong to a chess club.
    Men, **women**, and **children** play chess there.

These sentences have compound subjects made up of three subjects. Commas are used to separate the subjects, and the conjunction appears before the last subject.

Why are compound subjects useful? By putting similar ideas together in sentences, writers organize their thoughts and make their writing smoother.

Here are some examples of how you can put subjects together.

    Chess is a very old game.
    Checkers is a very old game.
    Chess and checkers are very old games.

    Joanna and Paul are good chess players.
    Maria is a good chess player.
    Joanna, Paul, and Maria are good chess players.

Compound Predicates

A **compound predicate** is made up of two or more predicates.

Subject	Predicate
Paul	calls Joanna and asks her to come over.
He	clears the table and sets up the game.

Both example sentences have compound predicates. That is, they each have two predicates. The two predicates are joined by the conjunction *and*.

Look at this sentence:

> The chess player **looked at the clock, studied the board,** and **made her move.**

This sentence has a compound predicate made up of three predicates. Commas are used to separate the predicates, and the conjunction appears before the last predicate.

Why are compound predicates useful? By putting similar ideas together in sentences, writers organize their thoughts and make their writing smoother. Look at these examples of how you can combine predicates.

> Paul won the first game.
> Paul lost the second game.
> Paul won the first game
> and lost the second game.

> They set up the pieces again.
> They played another game.
> They set up the pieces again
> and played another game.

See pages 66–67 for information on conjunctions and page 84 for information on punctuating nouns and verbs in a series.

Kinds of Sentences

Depending on what its purpose is, a sentence is one of four kinds: declarative, interrogative, imperative, or exclamatory.

A **declarative sentence** makes a statement.

> I saw a hippopotamus at the zoo.
> It was submerged in a large pond.

A declarative sentence ends with a period.

An **interrogative sentence** asks a question.

> What in the world is an okapi?
> Did you see a rhinoceros?

An interrogative sentence always ends with a question mark

An **imperative sentence** gives a command or makes a request.

> Don't frighten the monkeys.
> Show me the way to the walrus, please.

An imperative sentence ends with a period.

An **exclamatory sentence** expresses strong feeling.

> Watch how fast the penguins can swim!
> What a beautiful color the flamingos are!

An exclamatory sentence ends with an exclamation point.

Some sentences can be one kind or another. For example, *Look at me* can be either imperative (Look at me.) or exclamatory (Look at me!). *You will* can be either declarative (You will.) or interrogative (You will?). It depends on what meaning the writer intends. The meaning is indicated by the punctuation mark the writer chooses to use.

Where Is the Subject?

In a declarative sentence, the subject is usually found at or near the beginning. But sometimes writers place the subject in other locations.

> Aliens from outer space appeared in the movie.
> In the movie, aliens from outer space appeared.
> In the movie appeared aliens from outer space.

To find the subject of a declarative sentence, find the verb and add *who* or *what.*

> Who or what appeared? aliens
> *Aliens* is the subject.

In sentences beginning with *here* or *there,* the subject usually comes after the verb.

> There are our seats.   Here is the popcorn.
> Who or what are? seats   Who or what is? popcorn
> *Seats* is the subject.   *Popcorn* is the subject.

To find the subject of an interrogative sentence, change it to a declarative sentence, then find the verb, and ask *who* or *what.*

> Did Sean watch the movie?
> Sean did watch the movie.
> Who did watch? Sean
> *Sean* is the subject.

To find the subject of an exclamatory sentence, change it to a declarative sentence, then find the verb, and ask *who* or *what.*

> Wow, was that movie scary!
> That movie was scary.
> What was? movie
> *Movie* is the subject.

Where is the subject in this imperative sentence?

> Wait for me outside the theater.

Even though *you* does not appear in the sentence, it is understood to be the subject.

Nouns

What Is a Noun?

A **noun** names a person, a place, a thing, or an idea.

Everything has a name. Often something may have more than one name. A house is not just a house; it is also a building, a home, and a place. A woman is not just a woman; she may also be a doctor, a mother, and a golfer. All these words—*house, building, home, place, woman, doctor, mother, golfer*—are nouns.

A noun can name something that can be seen or touched, such as *tree, city, child,* and *star.* A noun can also name something that cannot be seen or touched, such as *laughter, greed, joy,* and *pain.*

Here are some more nouns:

Persons	Places	Things	Ideas
artist	farm	shirt	liberty
Chandra	Egypt	Great Wall	despair
student	continent	horse	humor
Darrell	Boston	Taj Mahal	happiness

A noun can be very general (*person, place, thing*), or it can be more specific (*boy, town, book*). Try to use more specific nouns in place of general nouns. It will help make your writing clearer and more precise. Compare these two sets of sentences:

The **boat** floated on the **water.**
The **animal** scampered up the **tree.**

The **canoe** floated on the **lake.**
The **squirrel** scampered up the **oak.**

The more specific nouns in the second set of sentences give the reader better, more detailed descriptions.

Common and Proper Nouns

A **common noun** names a general type of person, place, thing, or idea.

A dog may be a poodle, but so are a lot of other dogs. Because *poodle* is a name that can be applied to many dogs, it is a common noun. Common means "belonging to or shared by all alike." Other common nouns are *man, town, country,* and *building.*

A **proper noun** names a particular person, place, thing, or idea.

A dog may share the common noun *poodle* with many other dogs, but each dog also has a particular name, a name that is specific to it and to no other dog, such as *Jack, Flip,* or *Lady.* These names are proper nouns. Other proper nouns are *David Chang, New York, Japan,* and *White House.*

Proper nouns are always capitalized. Common nouns are not capitalized.

Here are some more examples of common and proper nouns:

Common Nouns	Proper Nouns
boy	Malcolm Ortiz
girl	Holly Jacobson
town	Des Moines
country	China
building	Sears Tower
ocean	Arctic Ocean
event	World War II
street	Maple Street
monument	Jefferson Memorial
newspaper	*The New York Times*

See pages 72–75 for information on capitalizing proper nouns.

Singular and Plural Nouns

A **singular noun** names one person, place, thing, or idea.

When a noun names only one person, place, thing, or idea, it is a singular noun. *Singular* means "being one, separate, individual." *Boy* names one person. *Hat* names one thing. *Boy* and *hat* are both singular nouns.

A **plural noun** names more than one person, place, thing, or idea.

When a noun names more than one person, place, thing, or idea, it is a plural noun. *Plural* comes from a Latin word that means "more." *Boys* names more than one boy. *Hats* names more than one hat. *Boys* and *hats* are both plural nouns.

Plurals of nouns are formed in several different ways.

1. Add -*s* to form the plurals of most nouns.

town	towns	dog	dogs	word	words
book	books	girl	girls	idea	ideas

2. Add -*es* to form the plurals of nouns that end in *s, sh, ch,* or *x.*

gas	gases	dish	dishes	match	matches
bus	buses	brush	brushes	box	boxes
dress	dresses	bench	benches	tax	taxes

3. When a noun ends in a consonant followed by *y*, change the *y* to *i* and add -*es* to form the plural.

penny	pennies	city	cities	enemy	enemies
baby	babies	fly	flies	country	countries

When a noun ends in a vowel followed by *y*, add *-s* to form the plural.

> essay   essays   monkey   monkeys   valley   valleys

4. For most nouns that end in *f* or *fe*, add *-s* to form the plurals.

> belief   beliefs   reef   reefs   cuff   cuffs   safe   safes
> chief   chiefs   roof   roofs   cliff   cliffs   fife   fifes

For some nouns that end in *f* or *fe*, change the *f* to *v* and add *-s* or *-es* to form the plurals.

> knife   knives   calf   calves   loaf   loaves
> life   lives   leaf   leaves   thief   thieves
> wife   wives   half   halves   shelf   shelves

5. When a noun ends in a vowel followed by *o*, add *-s* to form the plural.

> video   videos   studio   studios   stereo   stereos
> radio   radios   rodeo   rodeos   tattoo   tattoos

For some nouns that end in a consonant followed by *o*, add *-es* to form the plurals.

> hero   heroes   potato   potatoes
> echo   echoes   tomato   tomatoes

For music words that end in a consonant followed by *o*, add *-s* to form the plurals.

> alto   altos   concerto   concertos   piano   pianos
> solo   solos   soprano   sopranos   tempo   tempos

6. The plurals of some words are formed in ways that cannot be explained by a rule.

> child   children   goose   geese   tooth   teeth
> man   men   mouse   mice   foot   feet
> woman   women   ox   oxen

7. Sometimes the plural form of a noun is the same as its singular form. When you come across one of these nouns, the other words in the sentence should tell you whether the noun is singular or plural.

elk	elk	sheep	sheep	trout	trout
deer	deer	salmon	salmon	species	species
moose	moose	scissors	scissors	news	news

8. To form the plural of a closed compound word (a word made of two or more smaller words that has no space or hyphen between the words), add *-s* or *-es* to the last word.

spoonful	spoonfuls	workbench	workbenches
bookcase	bookcases	mailbox	mailboxes

To form the plural of an open (written as two separate words) or hyphenated (written with hyphen between the words) compound word, find the most important word and change it to its plural form.

fire engine	fire engines
sister-in-law	sisters-in-law
editor-in-chief	editors-in-chief

9. To form the plurals of numbers, letters, signs, and words used as words, add an apostrophe and an *s*.

It is easier to count by **2's**.
Charlene always forgets to dot her **I's**.
I made the **+'s** very large and black.
Alan has too many **and's** in that sentence.

See pages 90–91 for information on using apostrophes.

Knowing these rules can help you figure out how to form the plurals of nouns. But it is always a good idea to check a dictionary if you are not sure how to form the plural of a noun. Look for the plural form in the entry for the singular form of the word. If no plural form is shown in the entry, the plural of the word is formed simply by adding *-s*.

Possessive Nouns

The possessive form of a noun, called a **possessive noun,** is used to show who or what owns something. It can also show that the person or thing has parts.

Look at these sentences:

>The coat of Melissa is lying on a seat.
>Melissa's coat is lying on a seat.

Who does the coat belong to? It belongs to Melissa. Both sentences tell who the coat belongs to, but the first sentence sounds awkward. The second sentence sounds like something people might really say or write. *Melissa's coat* means

"the coat of Melissa," "the coat that belongs to Melissa," or "the coat that Melissa owns." By adding an apostrophe and an *s* to the noun *Melissa*, the writer created the possessive form of the noun— *Melissa's*—and used it to tell who owns the coat.

New York's subways are very crowded.
What do the subways belong to? New York
New York's is the possessive form of *New York.*

She stayed away from the platform's edge.
What is the edge part of? the platform
Platform's is the possessive form of *platform.*

The student's backpack was full of books.
Who owns the backpack? the student
Student's is the possessive form of *student.*

How to Make Singular Nouns Possessive

Add an apostrophe and an *s* to form the possessive of a singular noun.

Singular Noun	Possessive Form
city	city's
noise	noise's
James	James's
train	train's

How to Make Plural Nouns Possessive

Possessives of plural nouns are formed in two ways.

1. For a plural noun that ends in *s*, add an apostrophe at the end of the word.

Plural Noun	Possessive Form
tunnels	tunnels'
windows	windows'
riders	riders'
lights	lights'

2. For a plural noun that does not end in s, add an apostrophe and an *s*.

Plural Noun	Possessive Form
people	people's
children	children's
women	women's

It is important to place the apostrophe in the correct position in a possessive noun. The meaning of the possessive changes depending on the position of the apostrophe. For example, *the girl's money* means that the money belongs to one girl. *The girls' money* means that the money belongs to two or more girls.

See pages 90–91 for information on using apostrophes.

Verbs

What Is a Verb?

A **verb** tells about an action or a state or condition.

There are two kinds of verbs: **action verbs** and **state-of-being** (or **linking**) **verbs.**

Action Verbs

An **action verb** tells about an action.

> The pitcher **threw** the ball.
> Kelly **swung** her bat.

Not all action verbs, however, tell about such physical actions, or actions that can be seen. Some action verbs tell about mental or other less obvious actions.

> Kelly **knew** how to watch a pitch.
> She **thought** about her swing.

State-of-Being or Linking Verbs

A **state-of-being verb,** which is also called a **linking verb,** tells about a state or condition. This kind of verb tells what something is, or it links the subject to words that describe or identify the subject.

The most common linking verb is the verb *be* in all its forms: *am, is, are, was, were, be, being,* and *been.* Other common linking verbs are *appear, become, feel, look, remain, seem, smell, sound, stay,* and *taste.*

> The pitch **was** a high curve ball.
> It **seemed** higher than it really was.
> The **pies** taste good.

Some linking verbs can also be action verbs. Look at the sentence below.

> John **tastes** the pie.

Main Verbs and Helping Verbs

Look for the verbs in these sentences:

> Todd sweeps the floor.
> Janine makes the bed.

The verbs are *sweeps* and *makes*. Each verb is one word. But verbs can have more than one word.

> Todd **is sweeping** the floor.
> Janine **was making** the bed.

In these sentences, the verb is made up of two or more words. One word is the **main verb** and the other word or words are **helping verbs.**

Helping Verbs	**Main Verbs**
is	sweeping
was	making

Here is a list of the most common helping verbs:

be	do	can	may
being	does	could	might
been	did	will	must
am	have	would	
is	has	shall	
was	had	should	
were			

Some of these helping verbs can also be used as main verbs.

> Todd **has** the broom.
> Janine **is** in the bedroom.

The main verb and the helping verb do not have to be together in a sentence.

> Todd **did** not **sweep** the kitchen.
> **Is** Janine **putting** the sheets in the laundry basket?

Direct Objects of Verbs

A **direct object** receives the action of a verb.

With only a subject and a verb, a sentence can still express a complete thought and so be a sentence.

Claudia smiled.
Jeffrey laughed.

But often a sentence needs other words after the verb in order to express a complete thought.

Claudia took.　?　Claudia took the book.
Jeffrey told.　?　Jeffrey told me.

Book tells what Claudia took. Because *book* receives the action of the verb *took*, it is the direct object of the verb. *Me* tells whom Jeffrey told. Because *me* receives the action of the verb *told*, it is the direct object of the verb.

For a word to receive the action of a verb, the verb must have an action to send. It must be an action verb. A linking verb, which does not express an action, cannot have a direct object.

To identify the direct object in a sentence, find the verb and ask *whom* or *what.* The answer to the question is the direct object.

Jeffrey invited Claudia to a party.
Jeffrey invited whom? Claudia
Claudia is the direct object.

Claudia bought a gift for Jeffrey.
Claudia bought what? gift
Gift is the direct object.

Words After Linking Verbs

An action verb can be followed by a word in the predicate that receives the action of the verb. This word is called a direct object. Only an action verb can have a direct object. A state-of-being or linking verb cannot have a direct object. However, a linking verb can be followed by a word in the predicate that describes or tells about the subject of the sentence. This word is called a **predicate word.**

> The soup is **hot.**
> The bread is **fresh.**

In each sentence, a linking verb (*is*) links or connects the subject with a predicate word that describes or tells about the subject. The word *hot* describes the subject *soup.* The word *fresh* describes the subject *bread.*

A predicate word can be an adjective, a noun, or a pronoun.

> The baked chicken tastes spicy.
> *Spicy* describes the subject *chicken.*
> *Spicy* is an adjective.

> The green bean casserole is a new dish.
> *Dish* tells about the subject *casserole.*
> *Dish* is a noun.

> The most creative chef is she.
> *She* tells about the subject *chef.*
> *She* is a pronoun.

Only linking verbs can be followed by predicate words that tell about the subject. Remember, linking verbs are words such as *am, is, are, was, were, be, been, appear, become, feel, look, seem, smell, sound, stay,* and *taste.*

Subject-Verb Agreement

Remember, a singular noun names one person, place, thing, or idea.

cat   girl   book

A plural noun names more than one person, place, thing, or idea.

cats   girls   books

Just as nouns can be singular or plural, verbs can be singular or plural. Verbs must agree in number with the subjects in their sentences. "Agree in number" means that if the subject is singular, the verb must be singular, and if the subject is plural, the verb must be plural.

A **cat jumps** down.   The **cats jump** down.
The **girl plays** a game.   The **girls play** a game.
A **book falls** over.   Three **books fall** over.

In the example sentences on the left, the subjects *cat, girl,* and *book* are singular. The verbs *jumps, plays,* and *falls* are singular. The singular verbs agree in number with the singular nouns *cat, girl,* and *book.*

In the example sentences on the right, the subjects *cats, girls,* and *books* are plural. The verbs *jump, play,* and *fall* are plural. The plural verbs agree in number with the plural nouns *cats, girls,* and *books.*

You can find out more about the different forms of verbs on pages 29–33.

A few verbs and other words have special singular and plural forms that you need to remember.

Be, Do, Have

Some of the forms of the verb *be* are *is*, *are*, *was*, and *were*. The forms *is* and *was* are singular. The forms *are* and *were* are plural.

> The book **is** mine.   The book **was** mine.
> The cats **are** playing.   The cats **were** playing.

Two forms of the verb *do* are *does* and *do*. The form *does* is singular. The form *do* is plural.

> The girl **does** want that book.
> The girls **do** want that book.

Two forms of the verb *have* are *has* and *have*. The form *has* is singular. The form *have* is plural.

> The girl **has** a cat.
> The girls **have** a cat.

Here, There, Where

Some sentences begin with the words *here*, *there*, and *where*.

> Here are the cats.
> There is the girl.
> Where are the books?

Here, there, and *where* are not the subjects of the sentences. Find the subject by finding the verb and asking *who* or *what*. For example, who or what are here? The cats are. The word *cats* is the subject of the first sentence. Because the word *cats* is plural, the plural verb *are* is used in the sentence. Look at the second sentence. Who or what is there? The girl is. The girl is the subject of the sentence. The verb must agree in number with the subject.

Verb Tenses

Verbs have different forms, which are called **tenses**. These tenses are used to show time. Remember, verbs tell about an action or a state of being. Verb tenses are used to tell whether the action or state of being happened in the past, is happening in the present, or will happen in the future.

Present	I am a writer.	I **work** at home.
Past	I was there all day.	I **wrote** an article.
Future	I will be there tomorrow.	I **will call** you.

Present Tense

The **present tense** tells about an action or a state of being that is happening now.

To form the present tense:

• with a singular subject, add *-s* or *-es* to the base form of the verb—the form with no endings.

> George **repairs** cars.   He **fixes** the engines.

• with a plural subject, use the base form of the verb.

> The Goldmans **own** a restaurant.   They **serve** pizza.

• with the pronouns *I* and *you,* use the base form of the verb.

> I **manage** a store.
> You **design** houses.

Past Tense

The **past tense** tells about an action or a state of being that happened in the past.

To form the past tense of most verbs:

• add -*ed* or -*d* to the base form of the verb. Verbs that form the past tense in this way are called **regular verbs.**

repair	repaired	fix	fixed
own	owned	serve	served
manage	managed	design	designed

To form the past tense of other verbs:

• change the spelling of the verb. Verbs that form the past tense in this way are called **irregular verbs.** The spellings of the past tense forms of irregular verbs have to be memorized.

write	wrote	build	built
draw	drew	teach	taught
sell	sold	make	made

Future Tense

The **future tense** tells about an action or a state of being that will happen in the future.

To form the future tense of verbs:

• use the helping verbs *will* or *shall* with the base form of the verb.

paint	will paint	cook	will cook

Using More Than One Verb

When using verb tenses, the important thing to remember is to keep all the verbs in the same tense. For example, if one verb is in the present tense, then the other verb or verbs should be in the present tense, whether they are in the same sentence or different sentences.

Nina **typed, edited,** and **filed** medical reports.
(All three verbs are in the past tense.)

Ed **drives** a truck. He **makes** deliveries to stores.
(Both verbs are in the present tense.)

Parts of Verbs

Every verb has several different forms. Every verb also has three **parts**: present, past, and past participle. A verb's forms are made from these three parts.

Here are some examples of verbs and their parts:

Present	Past	Past Participle
work	worked	(have) worked
wash	washed	(have) washed
clean	cleaned	(have) cleaned
wrap	wrapped	(have) wrapped
dry	dried	(have) dried

The present part of a verb is the same as its present tense form. The future tense is formed using the present part and the helping verb *will* or *shall.*

The past part of a verb is the same as its past tense form. For most verbs, the past form is made by adding *-ed* to the present form. But if the present form of a verb ends in *y* or has a short vowel sound and a single final consonant, the spelling of its past form changes.

The past participle part of a verb is not the same as any one tense form. The past participle is used with helping verbs to form three additional verb tenses: present perfect, past perfect, and future perfect.

Present Perfect	has dusted	have scrubbed
Past Perfect	had dusted	had scrubbed
Future Perfect	will have dusted	will have scrubbed

All the examples on this page are regular verbs. Their past forms are made by adding *-ed* to their present forms, and their past forms are the same as their past participle forms. See pages 32–33 for information on the past and past participle forms of irregular verbs.

Irregular Verbs

Remember, regular verbs are verbs whose past forms are made by adding -ed to their present forms.

laugh	laughed	dance	danced
smile	smiled	walk	walked

Irregular verbs are verbs whose past forms are spelled differently from their present forms.

come	came	eat	ate
fly	flew	see	saw

With regular verbs, the past participle is the same as the past form.

play	**played**	(have) **played**
talk	**talked**	(have) **talked**

For some irregular verbs, the past participle is also the same as the past form.

bring	**brought**	(have) **brought**
hear	**heard**	(have) **heard**

But for many irregular verbs, the past participle is not the same as the past form.

sing	**sang**	(have) **sung**
write	**wrote**	(have) **written**

With both regular and irregular verbs, the past form is always used *without* a helping verb.

> Elena **grew** tomatoes and peppers in her garden.

With both regular and irregular verbs, the past participle is always used *with* a helping verb.

> Elena **has grown** tomatoes and peppers in her garden every year.

The following page lists the parts of many common irregular verbs. Use the list to check the forms of the verbs you write. Remember, a dictionary gives the parts of an irregular verb in the entry for the present form.

Parts of Irregular Verbs

Present	Past	Past Participle
begin	began	(have) begun
bring	brought	(have) brought
build	built	(have) built
choose	chose	(have) chosen
come	came	(have) come
do	did	(have) done
draw	drew	(have) drawn
drink	drank	(have) drunk
drive	drove	(have) driven
eat	ate	(have) eaten
fall	fell	(have) fallen
fly	flew	(have) flown
freeze	froze	(have) frozen
give	gave	(have) given
go	went	(have) gone
grow	grew	(have) grown
hear	heard	(have) heard
hide	hid	(have) hidden
keep	kept	(have) kept
know	knew	(have) known
make	made	(have) made
read	read	(have) read
ride	rode	(have) ridden
run	ran	(have) run
say	said	(have) said
see	saw	(have) seen
sell	sold	(have) sold
sing	sang	(have) sung
sit	sat	(have) sat
speak	spoke	(have) spoken
swim	swam	(have) swum
take	took	(have) taken
teach	taught	(have) taught
think	thought	(have) thought
throw	threw	(have) thrown
wear	wore	(have) worn
write	wrote	(have) written

Confusing Verbs

Writers often confuse these pairs of verbs. Learning the meanings of the verbs can help you use them correctly.

Bring–Take

Bring means "to come with or carry something from another place." *Take* means "to grasp" or "to carry away."

> bring, brought,   take, took,
> (have) brought   (have) taken
>
> Will you **bring** that plate to me?
> Please **take** a sandwich to Aunt Gertrude.

Can–May

Can means "to be able to." *May* means "to be allowed or permitted to."

> can, could   may, might
>
> Deborah **can** wiggle her ears.
> **May** I go swimming now?

Lead–Led

Lead (pronounced with a short *e* sound) is the name of a soft, heavy metal often used to make pipes. *Lead* (pronounced with a long *e* sound) is a verb that means "to show the way." *Led* is the past tense form of the verb *lead.*

> lead, led, (have) led
>
> This basket is as heavy as **lead.**
> Who will **lead** us to the picnic area?
> Jack **led** the children through the woods.

Let–Leave

Let means "to allow or permit." *Leave* means "to go away" or "to let stay as is."

> let, let, (have) let   leave, left, (have) left
>
> Molly **let** Karen choose a prize first.
> Michael won't **leave** until you do.
> Don't **leave** any food or trash behind.

Lie–Lay

Lie means "to rest" or "to be in a horizontal position." *Lie* cannot take a direct object. *Lay* means "to place or put down." *Lay* can take a direct object.

> lie, lay, (have) lain   lay, laid, (have) laid

> Will you **lie** down in the shade and take a nap?
> You can **lay** the newspaper over your face.

Rise–Raise

Rise means "to go upward." *Rise* cannot take a direct object. *Raise* means "to cause to go up." *Raise* can take a direct object. When the subject of the sentence is moving upward, use *rise.* When the subject of the sentence is making something else move upward, use *raise.*

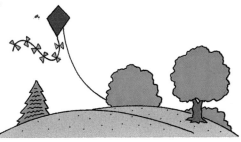

> rise, rose,   raise, raised,
> (have) risen   (have) raised

> David **raises** the kite high over his head.
> The kite **rises** high above the trees.

Sit–Set

Sit means "to occupy a seat." *Sit* cannot take a direct object. *Set* means "to put or place." *Set* can take a direct object.

> sit, sat, (have) sat   set, set, (have) set

> We **sat** on the grass to eat.
> Who **set** their dirty shoes on the blanket?

Teach–Learn

Teach means "to instruct or help to learn." *Learn* means "to gain knowledge."

> teach, taught,   learn, learned,
> (have) taught   (have) learned

> Allison **taught** the children how to play badminton.
> They **learned** the game very quickly.

Pronouns

What Is a Pronoun?

A **pronoun** is a word used to replace a noun. The noun that the pronoun replaces is called the **antecedent.**

Remember, nouns name people, places, things, or ideas. Pronouns can also be used to refer to these people, places, things, or ideas.

> **Celia** tried to catch **Celia's cat** so **Celia** could take the **cat** to the vet.

> Celia tried to catch **her** cat so **she** could take **it** to the vet.

Repeating the nouns in the first sentence makes the sentence very awkward. Replacing some of the nouns with pronouns makes the second sentence less awkward. *Her, she,* and *it* are pronouns. *Her* and *she* replace *Celia's* and *Celia. It* replaces *the cat.* The word or words a pronoun replaces are the antecedent of the pronoun. *Celia's* is the antecedent of *her. Celia* is the antecedent of *she. The cat* is the antecedent of *it.*

Sometimes the antecedent of a pronoun is another pronoun.

> Did Celia help **you** when **your** cat was sick?
> (*You* is the antecedent of *your.*)

Sometimes two or more nouns may be the antecedent of a pronoun.

> **Celia** and **David** take good care of **their** pets.
> (*Celia* and *David* are the antecedents of *their.*)

Sometimes the antecedent may be understood. It is not a word in the sentence, but the writer and reader understand who the antecedent is. In such cases, the antecedent is usually the person speaking.

> Bunky, a dachshund, is my favorite.
> (The antecedent of *my* is the speaker.)

Usually, a pronoun appears after the antecedent in the same sentence. But sometimes the pronoun appears in one sentence, and the antecedent appears in another sentence.

> The **kitten** is very playful. It chases its tail.
> (*Kitten* is the antecedent of *It* and *its.*)

Pronouns can be singular or plural. They can be used to refer to the speaker, to the person spoken to, or to the person, place, thing, or idea spoken about. (For more information on these ideas, see page 38.)

Singular Pronouns

Speaker	I	me	my, mine
Person spoken to	you	you	your, yours
People, places, things spoken about	he	him	his
	she	her	her, hers
	it	it	its

Plural Pronouns

Speaker	we	us	our, ours
Person spoken to	you	you	your, yours
People, places, things spoken about	they	them	their, theirs

Just as verbs must agree in number with the subjects of their sentences, pronouns must agree in number with their antecedents. When an antecedent is singular, use a singular pronoun. When an antecedent is plural, use a plural pronoun.

> The **cat** hid under the bed. **It** refused to come out.
> The **dogs** barked noisily. **They** heard something.

Personal Pronouns

The chart on page 37 lists personal pronouns according to their number (singular or plural) and their person. There are three persons: first, second, and third.
First person is the person speaking, or the speaker.
Second person is the person spoken to. **Third person** is the person, place, or thing spoken about.

First Person	Second Person	Third Person
I called.	You called.	They called.

Personal pronouns can also be grouped according to their **case.** There are three cases: nominative, objective, and possessive. A pronoun used as a subject in a sentence is in the **nominative** case. A pronoun used as an object is in the **objective** case. A pronoun that shows ownership is in the **possessive** case.

Nominative	Objective	Possessive
I saw Ann.	Ann saw **me.**	Ann is **my** friend.

Singular Pronouns

	Nominative	Objective	Possessive
First person	I	me	my, mine
Second person	you	you	your, yours
Third person	he	him	his
	she	her	her, hers
	it	it	its

Plural Pronouns

	Nominative	Objective	Possessive
First person	we	us	our, ours
Second person	you	you	your, yours
Third person	they	them	their, theirs

Personal pronouns change forms. They change forms to show number; to show first, second, or third person; and to show their use in a sentence.

Using Pronouns as Subjects and Objects

Pronouns as Subjects

The subject pronouns are *I, you, he, she, it, we,* and *they.*
When pronouns appear as the subjects of sentences or after
linking verbs, these forms are used.

Only subject pronouns can be used as the subject of a verb.

> After school Gerald went to his flute lesson.
> **He** has been taking lessons for a year.

> Janet hurried to soccer practice.
> **She** did not want to be late again.

Gerald is the subject of the first sentence. *He* is the subject
of the second sentence. The form *he* is used because it is a
subject pronoun. *Janet* is the subject of the third sentence.
She is the subject of the fourth sentence. The form *she* is used
because it is a subject pronoun. Pronouns such as *him* and
her could not be used as the subjects because they are not
subject pronouns.

Sometimes a pronoun appears as
part of a compound subject.

> Janet and **he** made the team.
> Gerald and **she** will
> play a duet.

Because the pronouns in the
sentences are part of compound subjects, the subject
pronouns *he* and *she* are
used.

To decide what pronoun
should be used, put each
part of the compound subject
in its own sentence.

> **Janet** made the team. **He** made the team.
> **Gerald** will play a duet. **She** will play a duet.

Then combine the subjects, keeping the same pronoun used
when the sentences were separate.

Sometimes a compound subject is joined by *or* or *nor.*

> Either **Janet** or **I** will be the goalie.
> Neither **Gerald** nor **she** can practice today.

To decide what pronoun should be used, use the same steps as with a compound subject joined by *and.* Leave out words such as *or, nor, neither,* or *either.*

> **Janet** will be the goalie. **I** will be the goalie.
> **Gerald** can practice today. **She** can practice today.

Then combine the subjects, keeping the same pronouns and putting back in the conjunctions.

Sometimes a pronoun is followed by a noun in the subject of a sentence. To decide what pronoun to use in the sentence, read the sentence, leaving out the noun.

> **We** soccer players are not afraid of hard work.
> **We** are not afraid of hard work.

> **We** flute players know all about hard work, too.
> **We** know all about hard work, too.

Subject pronouns are also used after linking verbs.

> **She** is an athlete.   An athlete is **she.**
> **He** is an artist.   An artist is **he.**

In the sentences on the left, *she* and *he* are the subjects. Therefore, subject pronouns were used. In the sentences on the right, the pronouns follow the linking verb *is* and identify the subjects *athlete* and *artist.* Therefore, the subject pronouns *she* and *he* were used.

Pronouns as Objects

The object pronouns are *me, you, him, her, it, us,* and *them.* When pronouns appear as the objects of verbs or prepositions in sentences, these are the forms that are used.

Unlike nouns, when pronouns are used as the objects of action verbs, they change their forms. *You* and *it* are used as both subject and object pronouns, but the other object pronouns are different from their subject forms.

Subject	Object
I	me
he	him
she	her
we	us
they	them

Only object pronouns can be used as the object of a verb.

Janet told Alice to kick. Janet told **her** to kick.
Gerald gave the music to Joe. Gerald gave **it** to Joe.

Sometimes a pronoun appears as part of a compound object.

The teacher asked Gerald and **him** to play.

To decide what pronoun should be used, put each part of the compound object in its own sentence. Then combine the objects, keeping the same pronoun used when the sentences were separate.

The teacher asked **Gerald** to play.
The teacher asked **him** to play.

Object pronouns are also used as objects of prepositions. A preposition is a word that relates a noun or a pronoun to another word in the sentence. The noun or pronoun that follows the preposition is called the object of the preposition.

The coach gave advice to Janet.
The coach gave advice to **her**.

See pages 60–65 for information on prepositions.

Possessive Pronouns

Like possessive nouns, **possessive pronouns** show owner-ship. The possessive pronouns are *my, mine, your, yours, his, her, hers, its, our, ours, their,* and *theirs.*

> **Your** coat is the same color as **her** jacket.
> **His** new shoes came from **my** shop.

The pronoun *your* tells who the coat belongs to. The pronoun *her* tells who the jacket belongs to. The pronouns *his* and *my* tell who owns the shoes and the shop.

Unlike nouns, pronouns do not form their possessives by adding an apostrophe and an *s.* Pronouns change their forms to show the possessive case. These forms never use apostrophes.

The possessive pronouns *mine, yours, hers, ours,* and *theirs* are used alone. *His* and *its* can be used alone or as adjectives. An **adjective** modifies, or describes, a noun or a pronoun. The possessive pronouns *my, your, her, our,* and *their* are used as adjectives.

> The hat is **mine.**   This is **my** hat.

(*Mine* tells whom the hat belongs to. It is used as a predicate word. *My* also tells whom the hat belongs to. It is used as an adjective. It modifies *hat.*)

Do not confuse possessive pronouns with contractions that sound similar but are spelled differently and, of course, mean different things.

Is this **your** glove?	(possessive pronoun)
You're missing one.	(contraction for *You are*)
The scarf has lost **its** fringe.	(possessive pronoun)
It's a very old scarf.	(contraction for *It is*)
I see **their** caps.	(possessive pronoun)
They're in that box.	(contraction for *They are*)

Indefinite Pronouns

Some pronouns do not refer to any specific person or thing. These pronouns are called **indefinite pronouns.** Because they do not refer to any specific person or thing, indefinite pronouns often do not have antecedents in their sentences. Sometimes their antecedents are people or things understood by the reader. Sometimes their antecedents are simply unknown.

Everybody enjoyed the art exhibit.
(*Everybody* has no antecedent.)

Many of the paintings came from other museums.
(*Many* refers to paintings.)

Here is a list of indefinite pronouns:

Indefinite Pronouns

Singular

one	anybody	something	other
anyone	somebody	nothing	another
someone	nobody	everything	one another
everyone	everybody	each	either
no one	anything	each other	neither

Plural

many	few	several
others	both	

Singular or Plural

all	some	any
most	none	

When using indefinite pronouns,

- use *his, her,* and *its* with singular pronouns.

    One of the men lost **his** ticket.
    Each of the women had **her** own tape recorder.

- use *his or her* if the person could be either male or female.

    Everyone moved at **his or her** own pace.

- use *their* with plural pronouns.

Demonstrative, Relative, and Interrogative Pronouns

Demonstrative Pronouns

Demonstrative pronouns are used to point out persons and things. The demonstrative pronouns are *this, these, that,* and *those. This* and *that* are singular pronouns. *These* and *those* are plural pronouns.

This is my sister.
That is my sister.

These are my sisters.
Those are my sisters.

This and *these* point out people or things that are close in space or time. *That* and *those* point out people or things that are farther away.

This is my brother.   That is my brother.

Relative Pronouns

A **relative pronoun** is used to introduce an adjective clause in a sentence. It connects the clause to the noun or pronoun the clause modifies. A clause is a group of words that has a subject and a verb but cannot stand alone as a sentence. The relative pronouns are *who, whom, whose, which, that,* and *what.*

Who, whom, and *whose* are used to refer to people. *That* is used to refer to things or people. *Which* and *what* are used to refer to things.

> The man **who** waved to us is my uncle.
> The cousin to **whom** I wrote a letter wrote back.
> The student **whose** essay won the contest is my sister.
> Dad read the book **that** was on the best-seller list.
> Aunt Joyce is the woman **that** brought the flowers.
> Mom likes green, **which** is also Dad's favorite color.
> A family dinner is **what** I'm looking forward to.

The noun or pronoun that the adjective clause modifies is the antecedent of the relative pronoun. For example, in the first sentence, the antecedent of the relative pronoun *who* is the noun *man.* In the second sentence, the antecedent of the relative pronoun *whom* is the noun *cousin.*

Interrogative Pronouns

Interrogative pronouns introduce questions. The interrogative pronouns are *who, whom, whose, which,* and *what. Who, whom,* and *whose* are used to refer to people. *What* is used to refer to things, places, or ideas. *Which* can be used to refer to people or things. Use *which* if the answer is a choice between two or more things.

> **Who** wants some of Uncle Paul's mashed potatoes?
> **What** is Aunt Stella bringing to the dinner?
> **Which** did you try—the green beans or the carrots?

An interrogative pronoun does not have an antecedent.

Subject-Verb Agreement

Indefinite pronouns and the pronouns *you* and *I* have special rules of agreement that you need to remember.

Indefinite Pronouns

Some indefinite pronouns are singular. They always use singular verbs. Some indefinite pronouns are plural. They always use plural verbs.

> **Everybody likes** to travel light. (singular)
> **Neither** of my bags **is** very heavy. (singular)
> **Both are** made of lightweight nylon. (plural)

Some indefinite pronouns can be singular or plural, depending on whether they are referring to one thing or several things.

> **All** of my money **is** in my tote bag. (one thing)
> **All** of my clothes **are** in my suitcase.
> (several things)

See page 43 for a complete list of singular, plural, and singular/plural indefinite pronouns.

You–I

Even though the pronoun *I* is always a singular subject, it uses plural forms of verbs. The only exceptions are the verbs *am* and *was*, which are singular verb forms.

> I **am** ready to go.   I **was** packed hours ago.
> I **travel** alone.   I **see** things.   I **meet** people.

Even though the pronoun *you* can be either singular or plural, it always uses plural forms of verbs.

> I said to the guide, "You **were** very helpful."
> I said to my fellow travelers, "You **were** very helpful, too."

Adjectives

What Is an Adjective?

An **adjective** is a word that tells about a noun or a pronoun.

Look for the nouns in these sentences.

> The children hike along the trail.
> The noisy children hike along the hot, dry trail.

Which sentence tells more about the children and the trail? In the second sentence, the word *noisy* tells about the noun *children,* and the words *hot* and *dry* describe the noun *trail.* Words such as *noisy, hot,* and *dry* that describe, or modify, nouns or pronouns are called adjectives.

Sometimes two or more adjectives modify the same word. You may have to separate the adjectives with commas.

> The **small, brown** lizard scurries under a rock.
> The lizard looks for a **cool, dark, hidden** hole.

Adjectives are usually placed before the word they modify. However, they may also be placed after the word they modify.

> The **tall, majestic** cactus stands alone.
> The cactus, **tall** and **majestic,** stands alone.

How Adjectives Modify

An adjective modifies a word by answering one of these questions about the word: What kind? How many? Which one?

- The adjectives in this sentence tell *what kind.*

> The **weary** hikers took off their **heavy** backpacks by the **cool** stream.
> (What kind of hikers? Weary ones. What kind of backpacks? Heavy ones. What kind of stream? A cool one.)

- The adjectives in this sentence tell *how many.*

> The hikers saw **six** snakes, **many** spiders, and **several** coyotes.
> (How many snakes? Six. How many spiders? Many. How many coyotes? Several.)

- The adjectives in this sentence tell *which one.*

> **That** hiker is making **her third** trip on **this** trail.
> (Which hiker? That one. Which trip? Her trip. Third trip. Which trail? This one.)

Remember, possessive pronouns are used as adjectives. They tell *which one* or *which ones.*

Proper Adjectives

Adjectives that are made by adding endings to proper nouns are called *proper adjectives.* Like proper nouns, proper adjectives are always capitalized. Like common nouns, common adjectives are not capitalized.

Proper Noun	**Proper Adjective**
New Mexico	New Mexican
America	American

Common Noun	**Common Adjective**
rock	rocky
beauty	beautiful

When a proper noun is used as an adjective, it is still capitalized.

> The trail led from the **Utah** border into the **Arizona** desert.

See page 17 for information on common and proper nouns and pages 72–75 for information on capitalizing proper nouns and adjectives.

Articles, Demonstrative Adjectives, Possessive Adjectives

Articles

The words *a*, *an*, and *the* are called **articles**. Articles always modify nouns. Therefore, articles are adjectives.

• *The* is used to refer to a particular person, place, thing, or idea. *A* and *an* are used to refer to one of a general group of people, places, things, or ideas.

> He caught the beetle. (a particular beetle)
> He caught a beetle. (any beetle)

• *A* and *an* are used with singular nouns. *The* can be used with either singular or plural nouns.

> a cricket   the ladybug
> an ant   the caterpillars

• Use *a* with words that begin with a consonant sound. Use *an* with words that begin with a vowel sound.

> a mosquito   a large moth
> an insect   an unusual fly

• Use *an* with words that begin with a silent *h*.

> an hour   an honor   an honest effort

Demonstrative Adjectives

This, that, these, and *those* are **demonstrative adjectives.**
They are used to point out people and things. *This* and *these*
are used to point out people or things that are close in space
or time. *That* and *those* are used to point out people or things
that are farther away. *This* and *that* are used with singular
nouns. *These* and *those* are used with plural nouns.

This butterfly is yellow.   **That** butterfly is orange.
These ants eat leaves.   **Those** ants eat seeds.

On page 44, *this, that, these,* and *those* were described as
demonstrative pronouns. These words can function as either
pronouns or adjectives. They are pronouns when they take
the place of nouns. They are adjectives when they modify
nouns by answering the question "Which one?"

This wasp is buzzing around my head. (adjective)
This is a problem! (pronoun)

Those wasps won't sting you.
(adjective)
Those are not the stinging kind.
(pronoun)

Possessive Adjectives

Possessive nouns were discussed as nouns
on pages 21–22, and possessive pronouns
were discussed as pronouns on page 42.
Both possessive nouns and possessive pronouns function as adjectives when they
are used to modify nouns and pronouns
in sentences. All possessive nouns can be
used as adjectives. Only the possessive pronouns *my, your, his, her, its, our,* and *their* can
be used as adjectives.

Alan's dream is to be an entomologist like **his** father.
(Possessive noun *Alan's* modifies noun *dream;* possessive pronoun *his* modifies noun *father.*)

Their study is about the **insects'** feeding habits.
(Possessive pronoun *their* modifies noun *study;*
possessive noun *insects'* modifies noun *habits.*)

Predicate Adjectives

A **predicate adjective** is an adjective that follows a linking verb and modifies the subject of the sentence.

Some adjectives follow a linking verb. Because these adjectives appear in the predicate of the sentence, they are called *predicate adjectives.*

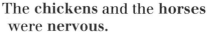

predicate

The animals seemed very **restless** today.

A predicate adjective describes the subject of the sentence. In the example sentence, the predicate adjective *restless* follows the linking verb *seemed* and modifies the subject *animals.*

One predicate adjective can modify a compound subject. Two predicate adjectives can modify a single subject.

The **chickens** and the **horses** were **nervous.**
(*Nervous* modifies *chickens* and *horses.*)

But the **cows** remained **calm** and **indifferent.**
(*Calm* and *indifferent* modify *cows.*)

Note that a predicate adjective comes after the word it modifies. (Most adjectives come before the words they modify.) The predicate adjective is separated from the subject by the linking verb and often by other words as well.

Remember, linking verbs are verbs that express a state or condition, not an action. Here are some common linking verbs:

am	was	become	remain	sound
is	were	feel	seem	stay
are	appear	look	smell	taste

See page 23 for information on linking verbs. See page 26 for information on words that come after linking verbs.

Comparing with Adjectives

Adjectives have two special forms that are used to compare things. The **comparative form** of an adjective is used when two things are compared. The **superlative form** of the adjective is used when three or more things are compared.

The dog is big. The elephant is big. The whale is big.

All three animals may be big, but some are bigger than others. To compare the bigness of the animals, use the comparative and superlative forms of the adjective *big*.

Use the comparative form *bigger* to compare two of the animals.

The elephant is **bigger** than the dog.
The whale is **bigger** than the elephant.

Use the superlative form *biggest* to compare all three of the animals.

The whale is the **biggest** of all three animals.

Endings *-er* and *-est*

• Add *-er* to make the comparative form of most short adjectives.

• Add *-est* to make the superlative form of most short adjectives.

Adjective	Comparative	Superlative
large	larger	largest
small	smaller	smallest
wet	wetter	wettest
fast	faster	fastest
dry	drier	driest
slow	slower	slowest

Notice the spelling changes that must take place in some adjectives before *-er* or *-est* is added. For an adjective that ends in *e*, such as *large*, drop the *e* before adding *-er* or *-est*. For an adjective ending in a short vowel and a single consonant, such as *wet*, double the final consonant before adding *-er* or *-est*. For an adjective that ends in a consonant and a *y*, such as *dry*, change the *y* to an *i* before adding *-er* or *-est*.

More and Most

- To make the comparative form of an adjective with two or more syllables, use the word *more* with the adjective.

- To make the superlative form of an adjective with two or more syllables, use the word *most* with the adjective.

Adjective	Comparative	Superlative
graceful	more graceful	most graceful
active	more active	most active
dangerous	more dangerous	most dangerous
intelligent	more intelligent	most intelligent

Irregular Forms

Some adjectives have comparative and superlative forms that are formed differently.

Adjective	Comparative	Superlative
good	better	best
bad	worse	worst
far	farther	farthest
many	more	most

See pages 57–58 for information on comparing with adverbs.

Adverbs

What Is an Adverb?

An **adverb** is a word that modifies a verb, an adjective, or another adverb.

Remember, an adjective modifies a noun or a pronoun. That is, it tells something about the noun or pronoun. An adverb modifies a verb, an adjective, or another adverb. It tells about the verb, adjective, or adverb.

> The carpenter looks **closely** at the wood.
> (*Closely* modifies the verb *looks.*)
> The old cabinet is **truly** beautiful.
> (*Truly* modifies the adjective *beautiful.*)
> She begins to clean it **very** carefully.
> (*Very* modifies the adverb *carefully.*)

Adjectives tell *what kind, how many,* and *which one* about the words they modify. Adverbs tell *how, when, where,* and *how much* about the words they modify.

> Sara works **patiently.**   (Works *how?* Patiently.)
> She will be finished **soon.**   (Finished *when?* Soon.)
> The cabinet stands **there.**   (Stands *where?* There.)

Adverbs that modify adjectives and adverbs usually come before the words they modify. Adverbs that modify verbs usually come after the verb, but they can be found in other locations in the sentence.

> **Now** the wood is old.   The wood **now** is old.
> The wood is old **now.**

Many adverbs are easy to identify because they have the ending *-ly.*

> slowly   finally   promptly   exactly

However, many adverbs do not have the *-ly* ending.

> almost   never   often   yesterday

Adjectives and Adverbs

Look at these two sets of words:

loud	loudly
slow	slowly
bright	brightly
sudden	suddenly
happy	happily
pleasant	pleasantly
beautiful	beautifully
furious	furiously

The two sets don't look very different from each other, do they? All the words are modifiers. The main difference between the adjectives on the left and the adverbs on the right is the words they modify.

Remember—

• **Adjectives** modify nouns and pronouns. They tell *what kind, how many,* or *which one* about the nouns and pronouns they modify.

• **Adverbs** modify verbs, adjectives, and other adverbs. They tell *how, when, where,* or *how much* about the verbs, adjectives, and other adverbs they modify.

How do you decide whether to use an adjective or an adverb in a sentence? Ask this question: "What word is being modified?"

The sun shone _____ in the sky.
<u>bright, brightly</u>

To choose between the adjective *bright* and the adverb *brightly,* ask what word in the sentence is being modified. The verb *shone* is being modified. Only adverbs can modify verbs, so the adverb *brightly* is the correct word.

After the shower, the flowers looked _____.
                                    beautiful, beautifully.

To choose between the adjective *beautiful* and the adverb *beautifully*, ask what word in the sentence is being modified. Notice that *looked* is used as a linking verb. A linking verb links the subject to words in the predicate that describe the subject. So the word being modified is the noun *flowers*. Only adjectives can modify nouns, so the adjective *beautiful* is the correct word.

Good–Well and Bad–Badly

In the pairs of words *good/well* and *bad/badly*, which are the adjectives and which are the adverbs? Writers and speakers often confuse these words.

• *Good* and *bad* are adjectives.

> The wet grass smells **good**.
> (*Smells* is used as a linking verb. *Good* is a predicate adjective.)

> Don't feel **bad** about the mud.
> (*Feel* is used as a linking verb. *Bad* is a predicate adjective.)

• *Well* and *badly* are adverbs.

> My new umbrella worked **well** during the rain.
> (How did it work? Well.)

> I **badly** needed a new umbrella.
> (How did I need? Badly.)

• When *well* is used to mean "healthy" and to describe a noun or pronoun, it is an adjective. In the sentence "I feel *well*," *well* is an adjective.

Comparing with Adverbs

Like adjectives, adverbs have two special forms that are used to make comparisons. The **comparative form** of an adverb is used when two actions are compared. The **superlative form** of the adverb is used when three or more actions are compared.

> Sam runs fast. Leon runs fast. Jose runs fast.

All three boys run fast, but they do not all run at the same speed. To compare the actions of the runners, use the comparative and superlative forms of the adverb *fast.*

Use the comparative form *faster* to compare the actions of two of the runners.

> Leon runs **faster** than Sam.
> Jose runs **faster** than Leon.

Use the superlative form *fastest* to compare the actions of all three runners.

> Of the three, Jose runs the **fastest.**

Endings -er and -est

• Add -*er* to make the comparative form of some short adverbs.

• Add -*est* to make the superlative form of some short adverbs.

Adverb	Comparative	Superlative
hard	harder	hardest
late	later	latest
soon	sooner	soonest
early	earlier	earliest

More and *Most*

• To make the comparative form of an adverb that ends in *-ly*, use the word *more* with the adverb.

• To make the superlative form of an adverb that ends in *-ly*, use the word *most* with the adverb.

Adverb	Comparative	Superlative
quietly	more quietly	most quietly
rapidly	more rapidly	most rapidly
happily	more happily	most happily
fearfully	more fearfully	most fearfully

Irregular Forms

Some adverbs have comparative and superlative forms that have nothing to do with adding either endings or words.

Adverb	Comparative	Superlative
well	better	best
badly	worse	worst
little	less	least
much	more	most

Many adverbs cannot be used to make comparisons. These adverbs do not have comparative and superlative forms. Often these adverbs answer the questions "Where?" and "When?" Examples include *here, there, inside, outside, everywhere, yesterday, today, tomorrow,* and *now.*

In autumn, we play **outside**. (*Where* do we play? outside)
Leaves are falling **everywhere**. (*Where* are leaves falling? everywhere)
Today, we'll play in Trini's yard (*When* will we play? today)

• When comparing the action of one person or thing to the actions of a group the person or thing belongs to, use the comparative form of the adverb and include the word *other* or *else.*

Jose runs **faster** than any **other** boy.
Jose runs **faster** than anyone **else** in the school.

See pages 52-53 for information on comparing with adjectives.

Double Negatives

Two negatives in the same sentence is one negative too many.

A negative is a word that means "no." Of course, the word *no* means "no." So do some words that have *no* in them.

nobody	no one	nothing
none	nowhere	not

But some negatives do not have *no* in them.

never	hardly	barely	scarcely

The negative word *not* is used in many contractions. In a contraction, *not* is spelled *-n't* and is combined with another word. This can make the *not* harder to see. Because *not* means "no," contractions with *-n't* are also negatives.

is + *not* = isn't
has + *not* = hasn't
are + *not* = aren't
can + *not* = can't
was + *not* = wasn't
could + *not* = couldn't
were + *not* = weren't
will + *not* = won't
do + *not* = don't
would + *not* = wouldn't
did + *not* = didn't
should + *not* = shouldn't
have + *not* = haven't

No Extra No's!

Two negatives in the same sentence is called a **double negative**. A sentence does not need more than one negative.

Incorrect	I **couldn't hardly** keep my eyes open.
Correct	I **couldn't** keep my eyes open.
Correct	I could **hardly** keep my eyes open.
Incorrect	I **haven't** done **nothing** all day.
Correct	I **haven't** done anything all day.
Correct	I have done **nothing** all day.

Prepositions, Conjunctions & Interjections

What Is a Preposition?

A **preposition** shows a relationship between words within a sentence. It relates a noun or a pronoun to another word in the sentence. The noun or pronoun that follows the preposition is called the **object of the preposition.**

The cat is **on** the **chair.**

In the example sentence, the preposition *on* shows the relationship between the object of the preposition *chair* and the noun *cat*. To see this relationship more clearly, try changing the preposition in the sentence.

The cat is **behind** the chair.　　The cat is **under** the chair.

Changing the preposition changes the relationship between *chair* and *cat*.

Common Prepositions

about	beneath	inside	since
above	beside	into	through
across	between	like	throughout
after	beyond	near	to
against	but	of	toward
along	by	off	under
among	down	on	underneath
around	during	onto	until
at	except	out	up
before	for	outside	upon
behind	from	over	with
below	in	past	without

Prepositional Phrases

In general, prepositions appear as part of prepositional phrases. A **prepositional phrase** is a group of words that begins with a preposition and ends with the object of the preposition. The object of the preposition may be a noun or a pronoun.

prepositional phrase

Denise is going away for the Memorial Day weekend.

preposition   object of
              preposition

prepositional phrase

The trip is an annual event for her friends and her.

preposition   object of
              preposition

Note that in a prepositional phrase, one or more words may come between the preposition and the object. In the first example sentence, *the* and *Memorial Day* describe the object *weekend.* Words that describe the object are part of the prepositional phrase. Also, a preposition may have more than one object. In the second example sentence, the preposition has two objects: the noun *friends* and the pronoun *her.*

A sentence may have more than one prepositional phrase.

> **In the morning, Denise will drive to a state park and camp for three days.**

Prepositional phrases may follow one another in a sentence. This sentence has three prepositional phrases in a row.

> **Her favorite camping place is in the woods by the river near the cliffs.**

Prepositional Phrases as Adjectives and Adverbs

Like adjectives and adverbs, prepositional phrases are used as modifiers.

A prepositional phrase that modifies a noun or a pronoun is called an **adjective phrase.** Like adjectives, an adjective phrase tells *what kind* or *which one* about the noun or pronoun it modifies.

> Novels **about faraway places** are Antonio's favorites.
> (*About faraway places* modifies the noun *novels*. The adjective phrase tells *what kind*.)

> He also reads books **from the travel section.**
> (*From the travel section* modifies the noun *books*. The adjective phrase tells *which ones*.)

A prepositional phrase that modifies a verb, an adjective, or an adverb is called an **adverb phrase.** Like adverbs, an adverb phrase tells *how, when, where,* or *how much* about the verb, adjective, or adverb it modifies.

> Antonio is happy **at the library.**
> (*At the library* modifies the adjective *happy.* The adverb phrase tells *where.*)

> Often he stays there and reads **for hours.**
> (*For hours* modifies the verb *reads*. The adverb phrase tells *how much.*)

> Antonio chooses his books **with great care.**
> (*With great care* modifies the verb *chooses*. The adverb phrase tells *how.*)

> He does most of his reading **on weekends.**
> (*On weekends* modifies the verb *does*. The adverb phrase tells *when.*)

See pages 47–48 for information on adjectives as modifiers and page 54 for information on adverbs as modifiers.

Pronouns After Prepositions

Remember, only the object forms of personal pronouns can be used as the objects of verbs or the objects of prepositions. The object forms are *me, you, him, her, it, us,* and *them.*

> Did Rachel give the letter **to him?**
> Ed said the letter was **for her.**
> I think the letter is **from them.**
> Quinn wants to take the letter **with us.**

Sometimes a preposition has more than one object. If any of the objects are pronouns, the object forms of the pronouns must be used.

> Trisha wrote a letter to Dad and **me.**
> The letter from **you** and **him** arrived today.

To decide which pronoun form to use in sentences with more than one object, read the sentence with only the pronoun after the preposition.

> Letters came from everyone but Jarod and _____.
> $\overline{\text{she, her}}$

> Letters came from everyone but **her.**
> Letters came from everyone but Jarod and **her.**

> I wrote back to Trisha and _____.
> $\overline{\text{he, him}}$

> I wrote back to **him.**
> I wrote back to Trisha and **him.**

See pages 40–41 for information on using pronouns as objects.

Understanding Prepositions

Preposition or Adverb?

Some words, such as *by, up, down, in, out, around, above, over, inside,* and *outside,* can be used either as prepositions or as adverbs.

> Kenji glanced **up** as Alicia walked **by**. (adverbs)
> He glanced **up** the street as she walked **by** the door. (prepositions)

> When I went **out**, the dog ran **inside**. (adverbs)
> When I went **out** the door, it ran **inside** the house. (prepositions)

> Hal looked **around** and then climbed **down**. (adverbs)
> He looked **around** the attic and then climbed **down** the ladder. (prepositions)

How can you tell whether the word is a preposition or an adverb? If the word begins a phrase and is followed by a noun or a pronoun, it is probably a preposition. A preposition is always followed by its object. If the word is used alone, it is probably an adverb.

See page 54 for information about adverbs.

Confusing Prepositions

Writers sometimes confuse the following pairs of prepositions, using one when they should use the other. The information and examples found on the next page can help you use the prepositions correctly.

Between–Among

Between is used to refer to two people, things, or groups.

> On the bus, Gerald sat between Kathy and Mark.
> The bus stalled between Adams St. and Monroe Blvd.

Among is used to refer to three or more people, things, or groups.

> Hannah wandered among the museum displays.
> Among the four of us, we saw all the major exhibits.

Beside–Besides

Beside means "by the side of."

> At lunch, Hannah sat beside Gerald.
> Kathy put her lunchbox on the seat beside her.

Besides means "in addition to."

> What are you having for lunch besides juice?
> No one besides Mark will eat tofu.

From–Off

From can mean "out of the possession of." *Off* does not have that meaning. Do not use *off* when you mean *from*.

Incorrect	Hannah got a dollar off Mark.
Correct	Hannah got a dollar from Mark.

In–Into

In means "within or inside something."

> Kathy saw dinosaur skeletons in the museum.
> Gerald has a dinosaur book in his backpack.

Into indicates movement from the outside to the inside.

> How did they get those skeletons into the museum?
> Gerald put the book into his backpack.

Conjunctions

What Is a Conjunction?

A **conjunction** is a word that is used to join words or groups of words.

Common Conjunctions

The most common conjunctions are *and, but, or, nor, so,* and *yet.* These conjunctions are used to join subjects, verbs, objects, and sentences and make them into compounds.

To make a compound subject:

> Barbara likes movies. Tim likes movies.
> Barbara and Tim like movies.

To make a compound verb:

> Barbara rents movies. Barbara buys movies.
> Barbara rents and buys movies.

To make a compound object:

> Barbara collects movies. Barbara collects CDs.
> Barbara collects movies and CDs.

When two sentences are joined by a conjunction to make a compound sentence, a comma is placed at the end of the first sentence before the conjunction.

To make a compound sentence:

> Barbara likes dramas. Tim prefers science fiction.
> Barbara likes dramas, but Tim prefers science fiction.

When three or more subjects, verbs, or objects are joined by a conjunction, commas are placed after all the items but the last one.

> Barbara, Tim, and Jeremy go to the movies together.
> Movies make them smile, laugh, or cry.

Conjunction Pairs

Some conjunctions are used in pairs to join words or groups of words. Here are these conjunction pairs:

either . . . or	not only . . . but also
neither . . . nor	whether . . . or
both . . . and	

Either Barbara **or** Tim will choose a movie.
They debate **whether** to go now **or** to wait until later.
Barbara **and** Tim like **both** westerns **and** comedies.
Neither she **nor** he likes horror movies.
They watch movies **not only** at theaters **but also** on TV.

Conjunctions and Clauses

Some conjunctions join main and dependent clauses in sentences. A **main clause** has a subject and a verb and can stand alone as a sentence. A **dependent clause** has a subject and a verb but cannot stand alone as a sentence.

Dependent clause	**After** the movie was over
Main clause	they went home
Complete sentence	**After** the movie was over, they went home.

Some conjunctions that begin dependent clauses and join them to main clauses are

after	as though	if	until
although	because	since	when
as	before	than	where
as if	even though	unless	while

When Jeremy comes over, we will watch a movie.
I chose the movie **while** I was at the video store.
Since I have a VCR, we met at my house.
Let me get the popcorn **before** we start the movie.

Interjections

What Is an Interjection?

An **interjection** is a word or phrase used to express strong feeling.

An interjection might be used to express surprise, horror, excitement, anger, joy, fear, amazement, pain, or disgust. Here are some interjections:

Oh!	**Ah!**	Well!	**Wow!**
Oops!	OUCH!	Help!	Hey!

An interjection used alone with an exclamation point is functioning as an exclamatory sentence. The interjections above are exclamatory sentences. Remember, an exclamatory sentence expresses strong feeling and indicates this by ending with an exclamation point.

Usually interjections are used as part of a sentence. Sometimes they are separated from the sentence by an exclamation point, a question mark, or a period. The first word of the rest of the sentence is capitalized.

> Not again! How could I be so clumsy?
> Really? You're sure it doesn't hurt?
> Great! I'm so relieved you're all right.

Sometimes interjections are separated from the rest of the sentence by a comma. The first word after the comma is not capitalized.

> My, that bread smells good!
> Hey, who took the last slice?
> Gee, you can't trust anyone around fresh bread.

Words that are commonly used as other parts of speech can be used as interjections. Adjectives, verbs, and adverbs, can all be used as interjections.

> Unbelievable! Did you see her last dive?
> Wait! The judges are giving their scores.
> Never! I can't believe there are no 6's!

See page 14 for information on exclamatory sentences.

Subject-Verb Agreement

Prepositional Phrases in Subjects

Sometimes the subject of a sentence may be followed by a prepositional phrase. Because the prepositional phrase is between the subject and the verb, and the object of the preposition is closer to the verb than the subject, writers often become confused. They mistakenly make the verb agree with the object rather than the subject.

The **price** of most daily newspapers **is** 50 cents.
The **necklace** with diamonds and pearls **costs** too much.

What is the subject of the first sentence? *Price* is. *Price* is singular, so the verb *is* is singular. *Of most daily newspapers* is a prepositional phrase. *Newspapers* is the object of the preposition *of*. It is not the subject of the sentence. The object of a preposition can never be the subject of a sentence. Similarly, *necklace* is the subject of the second sentence. The verb agrees with *necklace*, not with *diamonds and pearls*.

Compound Subjects with Conjunctions

When two or more subjects are joined by the conjunction *and*, use the plural form of the verb.

Ben and Ellen **are** newspaper reporters.
Ben, Ellen, and Theo **write** local news stories.

To make sure you are using the correct verb form, say the sentence using a pronoun for the subject.

They are newspaper reporters.
They write local news stories.

When two or more subjects are joined by the conjunctions *or*, *either/or*, or *neither/nor*, use the form of the verb that agrees with the subject that is closest to the verb. In other words, if the subject closest to the verb is singular, the verb is singular. If that subject is plural, the verb is plural.

The mayor or council members **are** speaking today.
Either a reporter or a photographer **is** at the meeting.
Neither her writing nor his photos **tell** the whole story.

Parts of Speech

Using Words as Different Parts of Speech

What part of speech a word is depends on how the word is used in a sentence.

> The skyscraper towered **above** our heads.
> The skyscraper towered **above**.

The word *above* is used as a preposition in the first sentence. But how is it used in the second sentence? It is used as an adverb.

> **That** building is the tallest in the world.
> **That** is a very tall building.

The word *that* is used as an adjective in the first sentence. But how is it used in the second sentence? It is used as a pronoun.

You already know that words such as *above* and *that* can be two different parts of speech. Many other words can function as more than one part of speech. How a word is used in a sentence determines what part of speech the word is.

Each year the city hosts a 10-kilometer **race.**

Runners **race** through the city streets.

How is *race* used in the first sentence? It is used as a noun. It names a thing and it receives the action of the verb *hosts.* How is *race* used in the second sentence? It is used as a verb. It expresses an action. Same word, two different parts of speech.

Mechanics

The word "mechanics" refers to capitalization and punctuation. Using capital letters and punctuation correctly in your writing will help you get your ideas across clearly.

Capital letters are very helpful to readers. They point out things such as the beginnings of sentences and the names of specific people, places, and things.

Punctuation marks are even more helpful. When we speak, we use pauses and changes in our voices to signal things such as the ends of sentences or the items in a list. In writing, punctuation marks take the place of those pauses and voice changes.

It makes sense to learn how use punctuation marks and capital letters correctly. Incorrect punctuation and capitalization will confuse or mislead your readers. When you use mechanics well, your readers get your meaning quickly and accurately, which, after all, is what you want.

This section explains the rules governing capitalization and punctuation in English. You will learn about the rules that must be followed and the situations in which the writer has a choice. The explanations are accompanied by examples to show you clearly when and how to use capitals and punctuation marks in your own writing.

Capitalization

Proper Nouns and Adjectives

Remember, a proper noun names a particular person, place, thing, or idea. A proper adjective is an adjective that is made by adding an ending to a proper noun. Proper nouns and proper adjectives are always capitalized. That is, they always begin with capital letters. Common nouns and common adjectives are not capitalized.

Common Noun	Common Adjective
city	urban
country	rural

Proper Noun	Proper Adjective
Paris	Parisian
China	Chinese

Proper nouns can be more than one word. Capitalize all the important words.

Gulf of Mexico   Declaration of Independence

Here are some rules for capitalizing words:

People's Names and Titles

• Capitalize the first, last, and middle names of people. Capitalize their initials, too. Remember to put a period after an initial.

Barbara Jordan
Ruth Bader Ginsberg
John F. Kennedy
J. Paul Getty
J.R.R. Tolkien
Susan B. Anthony

• Capitalize personal titles used with people's names. Capitalize a title whether it is written as a whole word or as an abbreviation. Remember to put a period after an abbreviation.

Mister Jorsky   Doctor Weiner   Professor Wong
Mr. Jorsky   Dr. Weiner   Prof. Wong

Captain Ellison   Senator Sanchez   Reverend Canby
Capt. Ellison   Sen. Sanchez   Rev. Canby

• Do not capitalize a title when it is used alone or after a person's name.

The doctor is with Jay Wong, professor of economics.
Ann Sanchez, senator from Arizona, is standing next to the captain.

• Capitalize these titles when they are used with names or when they are used alone to refer to the people who currently hold the positions.

the President   President Washington
(of the United States)
the Vice President   Vice President Johnson
(of the United States)
the Pope   Pope John Paul II

Pronoun *I*

• Capitalize the pronoun *I*.

Aunt Sue told me that I had grown.
She says that every time, and I just smile.

Days, Months, Holidays, and Seasons

• Capitalize the names of days, months, and holidays. Do not capitalize the names of the seasons.

The fourth Thursday in November is Thanksgiving.
Valentine's Day is Monday, February 14.
The Fourth of July is a major summer holiday.

Geographical Names

• Capitalize the names of places and things, including

Continents—North America, Asia, Europe, Africa
Countries—India, Canada, Spain, South Korea
States/Provinces—Oregon, Manitoba, Rhode Island
Cities/Towns—Tokyo, San Antonio, Moose Jaw
Mountains—the Rocky Mountains, the Himalayas
Oceans—Arctic Ocean, Pacific Ocean, Indian Ocean
Lakes—Lake Erie, Lake Victoria, Crater Lake
Rivers—the Nile River, the Amazon River
Parks—Zion National Park, Starved Rock State Park
Buildings—Empire State Building, Eiffel Tower
Streets—Madison Avenue, Sunset Boulevard
Highways—Interstate 57, Route 87, the Natchez Trace
Monuments—Lincoln Memorial, Washington Monument
Bridges—Golden Gate Bridge, Sydney Harbour Bridge

Nationalities, Languages, and Religions

Capitalize the names of nationalities, languages, and religions.

Mexican	Swahili	Islam
Irish	Gaelic	Catholicism
American	Yiddish	Hinduism

Religious Names and Terms

• Capitalize religious names and terms, such as names for God and religious writings.

God	the Lord	the Koran	the Vedas
Allah	Vishnu	the Bible	the Torah

Historical Events and Documents

• Capitalize the names of historical events and documents.

Battle of Gettysburg	Magna Carta
French Revolution	Voting Rights Act
Constitutional Convention	Treaty of Versailles
Crimean War	Bill of Rights

Businesses, Organizations, and Institutions

• Capitalize the names of businesses, organizations, and institutions, including schools, colleges, clubs, political parties, government agencies, and museums.

United Airlines	American Heart Association
Amoco Oil Company	National Geographic Society
University of Wisconsin	Rotary International
Cambridge University	Sierra Club
National Park Service	General Accounting Office
Smithsonian Institution	Democratic Party
Uffizi Palace	African National Congress

Planes, Trains, Ships, and Spacecraft

• Capitalize the names of planes, trains, ships, and spacecraft.

the *Spirit of St. Louis*
H.M.S. Victory
the *Twentieth Century Limited*
Galileo
the *Santa María*
Viking II

See page 17 for information on proper nouns, page 48 for information on proper adjectives, and pages 79–80 for information on punctuating abbreviations and initials.

First Words

Sentences

• Capitalize the first word of every sentence, whether the sentence is declarative, interrogative, imperative, or exclamatory.

> Many people think a robin is a sign of spring.
> How fast can a hummingbird fly?
> Please do not feed the toucans.
> What a beautiful color flamingos are!

Quotations

• Capitalize the first word of a direct quotation. A **direct quotation** is the repeating of a person's exact words. The first word of the quotation is capitalized.

> "Did you see that bird?" asked Emma.
> She exclaimed, "It was a scarlet tanager!"

• In a **divided quotation,** words such as *she said* or *he asked* divide the quotation into two parts. These words are called speaker's tags. The first word in the second part is capitalized *only* if it begins a new sentence.

> "I saw it," said Kate. "That bird was a cardinal."
> "A cardinal has red wings," argued Emma, "and that bird had black wings."

See page 14 for information on kinds of sentences. See page 87 and pages 92–93 for information on punctuating quotations.

Poems

• Capitalize the first word in each line of poetry.

> The Eagle
>
> He clasps the crag with crooked hands:
> Close to the sun in lonely lands,
> Ringed with the azure world, he stands.
> The wrinkled sea beneath him crawls:
> He watches from his mountain walls,
> And like a thunderbolt he falls.
> —*Alfred, Lord Tennyson*

Sometimes, particularly in modern poems, the lines of a poem do not begin with capital letters. To capitalize or not is the poet's choice. When you quote part of a poem, you should use the same capitalization that the poet does.

Outlines

• Capitalize the first word in every line of an outline. Capitalize the letters that indicate sections.

> Birds
> I. Kind of animal
>   A. Variety and range
>   B. Fossil history
> II. Structure and function
>   A. Feathers
>   B. Wings
>   C. Legs
> III. Behaviors
>   A. Mating and breeding
>   1. Territory
>   2. Nests
>   B. Feeding

Note that Roman numerals (I, II, III) indicate the major divisions, capital letters (A, B, C) indicate the next level of divisions, and Arabic numerals (1, 2) indicate the level of divisions after that.

To Capitalize or Not?

Titles

• Capitalize the first and last words of a title and all other words except articles, short conjunctions, and short prepositions such as *of, for,* and *with.*

> *U.S. News and World Report* (magazine)
> *All Quiet on the Western Front* (book)
> *A Raisin in the Sun* (play)
> *Dances with Wolves* (movie)
> "A Rose for Emily" (short story)
> "Nothing Can Stay Gold" (poem)
> "The Battle Hymn of the Republic" (song)

Family Relationships

• Capitalize words used to name family relationships *only* when they are used as names. Do not capitalize them if they follow an article (*a, an, the*) or a possessive adjective, such as *her* or *his.*

> Alex met Dad and Aunt Sue at the train.
> Alex met her father and her aunt at the train.

Sections vs. Directions

• Capitalize *north, south, east,* and *west* and their adjective forms when they refer to areas of the country or world. Do not capitalize the words when they refer to directions.

> Doug was born in the East but moved to the West.
> He liked Eastern cities but preferred the Western climate.
> To get to Phoenix, he traveled west on Interstate 10.
> It follows a southern route across the country.

See page 94 for information on punctuating titles.

Punctuation

Period

Here are some rules about when to use a period (.):

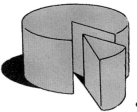

• Use a period at the end of a declarative sentence. Remember, a declarative sentence makes a statement.

We are making a casserole for dinner.
It has noodles, cheese, and broccoli in it.

• Use a period at the end of *most* imperative sentences. Remember, an imperative sentence gives a command or makes a request.

Hand me that cup of milk, please.
Set the temperature of the oven at 375°.

When an imperative sentence expresses strong feeling, use an exclamation point at the end of the sentence.

Be careful with the boiling water!

• Use a period after an abbreviation. Remember, an abbreviation is a shortened form of a word.

tbsp.	tablespoon	Jr.	Junior
oz.	ounce	St.	Street
Tues.	Tuesday	Ave.	Avenue
Sept.	September	hr.	hour
Dr.	Doctor	min.	minute

Some abbreviations do not have periods.

m	meter
g	gram
mph	miles per hour
AL	Alabama
KS	Kansas
VCR	videocassette recorder
FBI	Federal Bureau of Investigation

Some abbreviations may be written with or without periods. It is always a good idea to check a dictionary to see whether to use periods in an abbreviation. Also, except for a few abbreviations, do not use abbreviations in formal writing. However, you should use abbreviations for titles in formal writing.

• Use a period after an initial. Remember, an initial is the first letter of a name.

> Fannie M. Farmer   Fannie Merritt Farmer
> G. A. Escoffier   Georges Auguste Escoffier

• Use a period after each number separating items in a list.

> Shopping List
> 1. egg noodles, 10 oz.
> 2. shredded cheddar cheese, 6 oz.
> 3. fresh broccoli, ½ lb.
> 4. 2% milk

• Use a period after each number or letter separating items in an outline.

> Cooking
> I. Earliest types of cooking
>   A. Advances in cooking techniques
>   B. Cooking in ancient societies
>   1. Egypt
>   2. Greece
> II. Development of modern cuisines
>   A. Medieval cookery
>   1. Northern Europe
>   2. Italy
>   B. Emergence of French cuisine
>   C. Chinese influence
>   D. American cuisines
>   1. New foods
>   2. Technology

See page 14 for information on declarative and imperative sentences, pages 72–73 for information on capitalizing initials and abbreviations, and page 77 for information on capitalizing outlines.

Question Mark and Exclamation Point

Here are some rules about when to use a question mark (?) or an exclamation point (!):

Question Mark

• Use a question mark at the end of an interrogative sentence. Remember, an interrogative sentence asks a question.

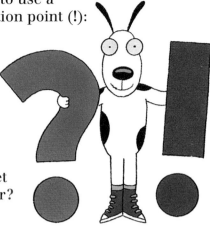

> How many games has this basketball team won?
> Did you see that last basket by Taylor?

Exclamation Point

• Use an exclamation point at the end of an exclamatory sentence. Remember, an exclamatory sentence expresses strong feeling.

> That was an incredible field goal!
> I can't believe the referee called a foul!

• Use an exclamation point at the end of an imperative sentence if the sentence gives a strong command.

Block that shot!   Stop that guy!
Get the ball back!   Don't miss!

• Use an exclamation point after an interjection. Remember, an interjection is a word or phrase used to express strong feeling.

Wow!   Great game!   Amazing!

See page 14 for information on kinds of sentences.
See page 68 for information on interjections.

Comma

Using Commas to Set Off

Commas (,) are used to set off a particular part of a sentence from the rest of the sentence. Setting off the part makes the sentence easier to read and understand.

Introductory Words

Use commas after words such as *yes, no,* and *well* when they are used at the beginning of a sentence.

> Yes, I did lose my favorite black pen.
> No, that black pen is not the one.
> Well, I have looked for it every-where.
> My, there are certainly a lot of pens in this office!
> Oh, I think I see my pen under that desk.

Direct Address

Use commas in **direct address,** that is, when someone is speaking in direct address. Place a comma after the name of a person spoken to when the name appears at the beginning of a sentence. Place a comma before the name when it appears at the end of a sentence. Place commas before and after the name when it appears in the middle of a sentence.

> Andy, did you take the last box of paper clips?
> There are plenty of paper clips in that drawer, Herb.
> But, Andy, do those clips have a plastic coating?
> You'll have to look at them, Herb, to see if they do.

Omitting the commas in direct address can affect the meaning of a sentence.

> Andy put the report in my office.
> Andy, put the report in my office.

The first sentence states an action that Andy has done. The second sentence is a request addressed to Andy. The comma makes the difference.

Appositives

Appositives add information about something in the sentence. An appositive
follows a noun and gives more
information about the noun.
Because they only add information, most appositives can be
taken out of their sentences without
changing the meaning of the sentences.

Use commas to set off most appositives.
Place a comma before an appositive at the end of a sentence.
Place commas before and after an appositive in the middle of
a sentence.

> Helen, our office manager, orders the supplies.
> She gets them from Elwood's, a local company.
> On Friday, the busiest day of the week, we always
> seem to run out of paper.

> Some appositives, however, are needed to make the
> meaning clear. These appositives are not set off
> with commas.

> The writer Nathaniel Hawthorne worked in
> an office.
> "How could he work and write?" asks my
> friend Amy.

Words and Phrases that Interrupt

Words and phrases such as *I think, however,* and *of course* are
called **interrupters** because they interrupt the flow of a sentence. They may be used at the beginning or in the middle of
a sentence. Use commas before and after interrupters.

> It would be hard, I think, to work full time and write.
> However, people have done both successfully.
> It would be easier, of course, to do one or the other.

Here is a list of some common interrupters:

after all	of course	indeed
by the way	for example	however
in fact	incidentally	therefore
I suppose	I believe	I think

Using Commas to Separate

Commas are used to separate words or ideas in sentences. These commas help readers more easily read and understand the sentences.

In a Series

Use commas to separate three or more items in a series. Place a comma after each item except the last one.

Glenn, Alicia, and Dave are planning a party.
They design, write, and send their own invitations.
They plan to have recorded music, videos, and games.

Omitting a comma in a series can affect the meaning of a sentence.

Carlos, Mary, Anne, and Dennis are coming.
Carlos, Mary Anne, and Dennis are coming.

In the first sentence, four people are coming to the party. In the second sentence, three people are coming to the party. A comma makes the difference.

With Adjectives

Use commas to separate two or more adjectives that modify the same noun.

Alicia wants to decorate with big, silver balloons.
Dave prefers to use long, colorful, plastic streamers.

Do not use a comma before the last adjective if that adjective is considered to be part of the noun.

But Alicia is a determined young woman.
(No comma before *young* because *young* is considered to be part of *woman.*)

Balloons will decorate the cold, dark basement walls.
(No comma before *basement* because *basement* is considered to be part of *walls.*)

In Compound Sentences

Use commas before conjunctions such as *and, but,* and *or* when these words are used to combine sentences.

> They can order pizzas, **or** they can order sandwiches.
> They talk about it, **and** they decide to order both.

To Include or Exclude

Use commas to separate information that is not needed to understand the sentence.

> Glenn, who has planned many parties, thinks this party will be a big success.
> Glenn is the only one of the three who has planned many parties.

In the first sentence, the clause *who has planned many parties* adds information to the sentence, but it is not necessary to the basic meaning of the sentence *Glenn thinks this party will be a big success.* So the clause is separated from the rest of the sentence by commas.

In the second sentence, the clause *who has planned many parties* is necessary. Without the clause, the meaning of the sentence changes. So the clause is not separated from the rest of the sentence by a comma.

To decide whether a clause should be separated by commas, try saying the sentence without the clause. If the sentence still makes sense, the clause probably needs commas.

To Make Meaning Clear

Use commas to make the meaning of a sentence clear and to avoid confusing the reader.

> When he called Glenn wanted to talk about the music.
> When he called, Glenn wanted to talk about the music.

> He had his CDs and his player was in the car.
> He had his CDs, and his player was in the car.

In each example, a comma keeps the reader from misreading the sentence and helps make the meaning clear.

Conventional Uses of Commas

Sometimes, using commas does not have much to do with meaning. In these cases, it is customary in English to use a comma in a certain place. These are **conventional** uses of commas. It is important for you to understand the conventional use of commas. Your readers expect to see commas in certain places and will be distracted if commas are not used correctly in these situations.

Dates

Use commas between the parts of a date. Place a comma before the year.

Pablo was born in Los Angeles on April 10, 1968.

On August 16, 1974, his family moved to Canada.

Pablo remembers November 2, 1974, very well because that was the day he saw snow for the first time.

Note that when a date appears in the middle of a sentence, a comma is also placed after the year.

No comma is used if the date has only a month and a year.

They moved back to the United States in May 1980.

Addresses

Use commas between parts of addresses. Place a comma between the name of a city or town and the name of a state or country.

Los Angeles, California   Toronto, Canada

When an address appears in a sentence, place a comma after each part except between the name of the state and the ZIP code.

Pablo went to college in Chicago, Illinois, and medical school in Miami, Florida. Now his mail is addressed to Dr. Pablo J. Herrera, 560 14th Street, Brooklyn, NY 11218.

Letters

Use a comma after the greeting in a friendly letter. Use a comma after the closing in a friendly or business letter.

Dear Pablo,	Dear Mama,
Love,	Your son,
Sincerely yours,	Respectfully,

Dear Pablo,

Love,
Mama

Quotations

Use commas to set off speaker's tags from direct quotations.

Remember, a **direct quotation** is the repeating of a person's exact words. Quotation marks are placed before and after the quotation. Phrases such as *he said* and *she asked* are called **speaker's tags.**

Mama asked, "When are you coming for a visit?"
"I'll come for your birthday," Pablo replied.

In the first sentence, the speaker's tag *Mama asked* is at the beginning of the sentence. So a comma is placed after the last word of the speaker's tag. In the second sentence, the speaker's tag *Pablo replied* is at the end of the sentence. So a comma is placed between the last word of the quotation *and* the closing quotation mark.

In a divided quotation, the speaker's tag divides the quotation into two parts.

"My birthday," said Mama, "is three months away."

A comma is placed after the last word in the first part of the quotation *and* inside the quotation marks. A comma is also placed after the last word of the speaker's tag.

You can learn more about punctuating quotations on pages 92–93. See page 76 for information on capitalizing quotations.

Semicolon and Colon

Semicolons (;), like commas, separate parts of sentences. But a semicolon indicates a more definite break than a comma does. Colons (:) signal an even stronger break. A colon usually points to what comes next.

Semicolon

• Use a semicolon between two related sentences.

Two related sentences can be combined using a comma and a conjunction such as *and, but,* or *or.* The sentences can also be combined using a semicolon. The semicolon takes the place of the comma and the conjunction.

> Chris tosses the ball up, **and** her racquet smacks it hard.
> Chris tosses the ball up; her racquet smacks it hard.

> The ball goes right to Ivan, **but** he swings and misses it.
> The ball goes right to Ivan; he swings and misses it.

• Use semicolons and certain conjunctions between two related sentences.

Two related sentences can be combined using one of the following conjunctions: *accordingly, also, besides, furthermore, however, instead, moreover, nevertheless, otherwise, therefore.* A semicolon is placed before the conjunction, and a comma is placed after the conjunction.

> Ivan has a good backhand; **however,** he needs to work on his serve.
> Chris has a powerful serve; **furthermore,** she rarely hits the ball into the net.

• Use semicolons between items in a series when there are commas in the items.

> Spectators at the game include Chris's mother, who is also a tennis player; Ivan's father, who once played at Wimbledon; and Ivan's younger brother.

Colon

• Use a colon after the greeting in a business letter.

> Dear Sir:　　Dear Mrs. Tanaka:
> Dear Customer Service Representative:

• Use a colon between the numbers for hours and minutes in a time expression.

> 8:15 A.M.　　　　12:05 P.M.　　　　10:28 P.M.

The abbreviations *A.M.* and *P.M.*, which are used in time expressions, stand for *ante meridiem,* meaning "before noon," and *post meridiem,* meaning "after noon." Capitalize both letters and put a period after each letter.

• Use a colon before a list of items. The colon indicates "note what follows."

Usually, the colon follows a noun or a pronoun. Do not use a colon after a verb or a preposition that introduces a list.

> Chris packed a can of tennis balls, an extra pair of socks, a towel, and a water bottle in her gym bag.

> Chris packed the following items in her gym bag: a can of tennis balls, an extra pair of socks, a towel, and a water bottle.

> Before a match, Ivan does these activities: leg stretches, curl-ups, bicep curls, and deep breathing exercises.

> Before a match, Ivan likes to stretch his legs, do curl-ups and bicep curls, and practice deep breathing.

See page 85 for information on using commas in compound sentences. See page 87 for information on punctuating the closing in a business letter.

Apostrophe and Hyphen

Apostrophe

• Use apostrophes to form the possessive forms of nouns.

For a singular noun, add an apostrophe and an *s* at the end of the noun.

Heather's apartment	Boss's doghouse
the van's carport	the bus's garage

For a plural noun that ends in *s*, add an apostrophe.

the Garcias' ranch	the Larsons' farm
the frogs' pond	the lions' den

For a plural noun that does not end in *s*, add an apostrophe and an *s*.

the people's houses	the children's cabins
the geese's nest	the oxen's barn

• For more than one noun, add an apostrophe and an *s* to the second noun if both nouns have ownership of the thing that is possessed. In the examples below, both Andy and Beth have the same dog. Grandma and Grandpa have the same house.

Andy and Beth's dog	Grandma and Grandpa's house

If the nouns have ownership of different things, add an apostrophe and an *s* to both nouns.

In the examples below, Stephen and Cathy have different dogs. Aunt Mia and Aunt Janet do not have the same house.

Stephen's and	Aunt Mia's and Aunt
Cathy's dogs	Janet's houses

• Use apostrophes to form the plurals of numbers, letters, signs, and words used as words.

To form these plurals, add an apostrophe and an *s*.

8's, not 3's	dot the *i*'s and *j*'s
+'s and -'s	no *if*'s, *and*'s, or *but*'s

• Use apostrophes in contractions.

A contraction is made of two words joined together with one or more letters left out. An apostrophe shows where the letter or letters have been omitted. Here is a list of common contractions:

I am—I'm	you have—you've	can not—can't
you are—you're	she had—she'd	do not—don't
it is—it's	we will—we'll	did not—didn't
we are—we're	is not—isn't	has not—hasn't
they are—they're	are not—aren't	have not—haven't
I have—I've	was not—wasn't	will not—won't

Hyphen

• Use hyphens in compound numbers from twenty-one to ninety-nine and in fractions.

> thirty-one cousins   eighty-six votes
> two-thirds of the relatives   one-eighth of the voters

• Use hyphens in some compound words.

A **compound word** is made up of two or more smaller words. Some compound words are written as one word, some are written as separate words, and some are written with hyphens between the words. Look up a compound word in a dictionary to see whether it needs a hyphen.

> Our great-aunt lives with my brother and sister-in-law. Even though she is now the ex-mayor, she has not lost her self-confidence.

• Use hyphens to divide words at the end of lines.

When dividing a word at the end of a line, place a hyphen after the first part of the word and then write the second part of the word on the next line. Always divide the word between syllables. Do not divide a one-syllable word. Use a dictionary to find out how a word is divided into syllables.

> At 82, she worked harder than many younger candidates did on the campaign trail.

Quotation Marks

When you write what someone has said, you are quoting the person or writing a **quotation.** If you write exactly what the person says, you are writing a **direct quotation.**
If you do not write exactly what the person says, you are writing an **indirect quotation.**

Direct Quotations	She said, "I want to go."
	He asked, "Why do you want to go?"
Indirect Quotations	She said that she wanted to go.
	He asked why she wanted to go.

In a direct quotation, quotation marks are used to show which words the person said. A phrase such as *she said* or *he asked* used in a direct quotation is called a **speaker's tag.** No quotation marks are used in an indirect quotation.

• Use quotation marks before and after the words of a direct quotation.

Sheila declared, "The amusement park would be fun."
    "I'm not so sure about that," Bert groaned.

• When the speaker's tag is at the beginning of a sentence, a comma is placed after the speaker's tag.

Sheila said, "I like the really fast, high rides."
    Bert muttered, "I like the slow, low ones."

• When the speaker's tag is at the end of the sentence, a comma is placed after the quotation inside the quotation marks.

"I've seen you ride the roller coaster," insisted Sheila.
"You've seen me ride it only once," replied Bert.

• When a quotation is at the end of a sentence, and the quotation ends with a period, question mark, or exclamation point, place the end punctuation mark inside the quotation marks.

> Sheila said, "I could ride it again and again."
> She asked, "Why don't you like the fast rides?"
> Bert answered, "Because they make me sick!"

• When a quotation is at the beginning of a sentence, and the quotation ends with a question mark or an exclamation point, place the end punctuation mark inside the quotation marks.

> "Did they make you dizzy and queasy?" asked Sheila.
> "But that's why the rides are fun!" she exclaimed.

• When a question mark or an exclamation point belongs to the sentence and *not* to the quotation, place the end punctuation mark outside the quotation marks.

> Did Bert actually say, "You're crazy, Sheila"?
> How astounding to hear Bert say, "OK, I'll go"!

A direct quotation that is divided into two parts is called a **divided quotation.** In a divided quotation, the speaker's tag is in the middle of the quotation.

> "Sitting in the front seat of the first car," **said Sheila,** "is the only way to ride a roller coaster!"
> "My head hurts," **moaned Bert.** "I think I left my stomach somewhere back on the first loop."

Quotation marks are used to mark both parts of the quotation. A comma is placed after the words in the first part of the quotation. In the first example sentence, a comma is placed after the speaker's tag because the second part of the quotation is *not* a new sentence. In the second example sentence, a period is placed after the speaker's tag because the second part of the quotation is a new sentence.

See page 76 for information on capitalizing direct quotations and page 87 for information on using commas in direct quotations.

Punctuating Titles

• Use quotation marks around the titles of short stories, poems, songs, essays, chapters of books, and articles in magazines or newspapers.

> "The Tell-Tale Heart" (short story)
> "Ode to the West Wind" (poem)
> "Auld Lang Syne" (song)
> "Civil Disobedience" (essay)
> Chapter 3, "The Solar System" (chapter)
> "Vietnam: The Ascending Dragon" (article)

When a title is written in a sentence, a period or comma after the title is placed inside the quotation marks. A semicolon or colon is placed outside the quotation marks.

> Our assignment is to read Chapter 4, "The Earth."
> Read "The Cask of Amontillado"; it is a scary story.

If a question mark or an exclamation point is part of a title, it is placed inside the quotation marks. If the question mark or exclamation point is not part of a title, it is placed outside the quotation marks.

> The funniest article in the magazine was "Help! I'm Caught in the Internet!"
> Did you read the humorous essay "You Can't Catch a Computer Virus"?

• Underline the titles of books, magazines, newspapers, plays, movies, and TV series.

> Sarah, Plain and Tall (book)
> Newsweek (magazine)
> The Wall Street Journal (newspaper)
> Romeo and Juliet (play)
> Raiders of the Lost Ark (movie)
> The Brady Bunch (TV series)

In printed materials, these titles appear in **italics.** Italics are slanted letters: *Beauty and the Beast.*

See page 78 for information on capitalizing titles.

Writing

Every writer has his or her own ways of writing. But to be able to talk about writing, it is necessary to choose one possible way to write, even as we recognize that writing is different for every writer and indeed for every kind of writing.

In this section, we will first discuss the writing process. By breaking the process into five possible stages, we can talk about what is involved in writing, from the idea to the finished product. The section explains these stages of the writing process, stressing how the stages are related to each other. Actually, the stages of writing function more like a circle (each stage leading back as well as forward) than a line (each stage as one definite step). We will offer help and suggestions in everything from finding ideas to writing a good beginning to sharing your writing with others. Use these suggestions if you need to. In time and with practice, you will discover your own ways of writing.

You will also learn some skills that can be useful when writing or working on any assignment. Finding the right word when you are writing can be very important. A dictionary or a thesaurus can be helpful in this quest. This section discusses how to use both of these reference sources. Spelling words correctly is also an important writing skill. We suggest ways you can improve your spelling ability, from keeping a list of troublesome words to remembering a few key rules. You will also find a list of some commonly confused words with meanings and sentences to help you use the words correctly.

The Writing Process

Five Stages of the Writing Process

Words like "process" and "stages" may make writing sound like something very mechanical. Actually, writing is anything but mechanical. But the idea of a process and stages helps when discussing what is involved in writing. Usually, the stages come up in the following order.

Prewriting. *The writer looks for a topic to write about and information on the topic.* Prewriting, as the name says, takes place *before* any writing. The task at this stage is to decide what you want to write about. Do anything that helps you make that choice. Perhaps you get ideas from reading, playing music, doodling on paper, or talking to someone.

Drafting. *The writer puts his or her ideas down on paper.* When writing a draft, you let your ideas flow and see what happens. Concentrate on getting down what you want to say. When you have finished a draft, put it aside and look at it again later. Also, having others read or listen to your draft can be helpful.

Revising. *The writer tries to improve what he or she has written.* Based on your own evaluation or the responses of others, you may decide to add or take out information, change the order of sentences or paragraphs, or replace words.

Proofreading. *The writer checks his or her writing for errors in spelling, punctuation, capitalization, and grammar.* Now that you have finished your revisions, it is time to look for and correct spelling errors and other mistakes before making your final copy.

Publishing. *The writer shares his or her writing with an audience.* Written form is only one of the ways to publish your writing.

Prewriting

How to Get an Idea

Some writers think this is the most difficult stage in the writing process. "What do I write about?" On the one hand, the possibilities are endless. On the other hand, that thought is not very comforting . . . or helpful. The task is to choose among all those possible topics and to do so wisely, carefully, and appropriately. But how?

1. Ideas for writing can come from many places and in many ways. First, look around you. The old saying "Write about what you know" has some truth in it. Ideas for writing can come from the everyday experiences you have with family and friends, with people you meet, with activities you do, with events and places you see. Make a list of favorite people, places, and things. Think about your favorite hobbies, activities, or skills. What is something you know how to do well and could explain to others? Have you recently read a story, book, or poem that made an impression on you?

2. You can write about past experiences or memories. If you keep a journal, it can be a good source for memory ideas. Look through old photographs or talk to family members to see what kinds of memories you can recall.

3. Read newspapers and magazines. Listen to the radio and television. Pay attention to what is going on in your community, in your state, in the nation, and in the world.

4. Try writing down anything that comes to mind. No matter how silly or useless your writing may seem, keep putting the words on paper as they flow through your head. When you go back and read what you wrote, you may find an idea there.

5. Talk with others about your ideas. Just hearing yourself say your ideas out loud may help you decide whether they seem like good writing topics or not. Try the ideas out on classmates, friends, or family members. They may be able to offer suggestions.

6. You might be able to use a graphic aid or some kind of visual device to help you find a topic. Try drawing a picture, diagram, map, chart, or idea web.

You use an **idea web** to make connections between ideas. In the center of your paper, write a possible subject and circle it. Then write any related ideas around the center circle. Circle them and draw lines from those circles to the center circle. Continue to add as many circles and lines as you wish. Your idea web can help you identify writing topics related to your original subject that may be a more usable size. (Later, you can also use your web to think of details about your topic.)

You can make a list based on the same concept as the idea web. Write a possible subject; then list examples or details related to the subject. From that list, choose one item and make another list of details. Again, this process can not only help you find a writing topic in a broad subject, but also show you whether you have enough details to begin writing.

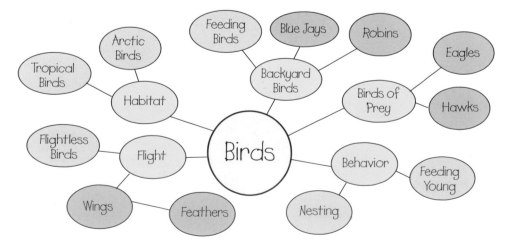

You can use a chart to think of ideas. Perhaps you are thinking about writing a description. Write a possible subject at the top of the chart; then make five columns, one for each sense. Write appropriate details in each column. Writing the details may give you an idea for a topic. Or, as with the idea web, the chart can be used to provide details for your later writing.

7. Ask yourself questions about a subject. See if you can get a personal angle on the subject by answering these questions: "Why do I want to write about this? What do I know about it? What do I want to know about it?"

Try asking *who, what, where, when, why,* and *how* questions about a subject. Questions, like graphic aids, can help you see the parts of a subject so that you can decide which part or parts you want to write about.

8. Whatever methods you use to generate ideas for topics, try to choose a topic that matters to you. The whole writing process will be much more interesting, exciting, and worthwhile if you choose something you care about or that interests you. It doesn't have to be something you like or enjoy; it could be something you dislike or that angers you.

Think of something you feel angry, sad, or joyful about. Think of an important or difficult problem or issue you have faced. Did you find a solution? If so, telling about the problem and solution might be helpful to others. The important thing is to be involved in the topic you write about.

9. Prepare for future writing by collecting ideas all the time. Save that list of favorite people, places, and things you made. Clip interesting newspaper and magazine articles. Jot down anything that might be of use later. Put these items in a notebook or folder to use the next time you need an idea for writing.

How to Develop a Topic

You have chosen your topic. Now what do you do? You start collecting lots of supporting details for your topic. There are different kinds of supporting details. The ones you use depend on what you are writing.

Facts. A **fact** is anything that can be proved true. An **opinion** is something that cannot be proved true. "The White House is located at 1600 Pennsylvania Avenue" is a fact. The location can be checked and proved to be true. "The White House is a very beautiful building" is an opinion. Whether it is beautiful or not cannot be proved true. How can facts be proved true? They can be checked in reference sources, such as encyclopedias. When you write, you use facts to support your main idea.

Reasons. These are logical explanations or arguments that you use to support your opinion. For example, if you think a historical building should be saved, you might explain how the building could be used, argue the importance of keeping some things from the past, and point out the value of the building as a tourist attraction.

Examples. These are instances of something that you use to support a point. For example, in your campaign to save the historical building, you might offer examples of historical buildings saved in other cities and how they proved to be beneficial to the cities.

Sensory details. These tell how things look, taste, feel, smell, and sound. They are most often used in descriptions. For example, in a description of an old building, you might describe how the rooms look and smell, how the floors creak, and how the woodwork feels.

Stories or events. You can tell a particular story or describe a particular event to support a point. The story or event may be from your own or others' experiences. It may be from your reading or your imagination. For example, in your campaign to save the historical building, you might tell the story of the building's architect or describe a president's historic visit to the building.

Where do all these details come from? First, look back at the prewriting you did when you were exploring your topic. In your notes, lists, charts, and webs, you will probably find many details.

But what if you still do not have enough details? How do you get more details? Here are some suggestions:

Research. Go to the library. Look in books, magazines, encyclopedias, and other reference sources. For much of the writing you do, research will be your primary source of details.

Interview. Get information from other people. For a description of a party, this might be some of the people who attended the party. For a report on snakes, this might be the keeper at the zoo's reptile house and a herpetologist (a person who studies reptiles and amphibians).

Observe. Look at things closely and describe them carefully. How does a snake move?

Remember. Think about what you can recall from your own experience. Have you ever encountered any snakes?

Imagine. Use your imagination. What do you think it would be like to be a snake?

The details you find may make you want to change your topic. You may find something that you think would be even more interesting to write about than your first topic idea. Such adjustments are a natural part of the writing process, especially during the prewriting stage. Go ahead and change your idea; then begin a new list of details.

Reason for Writing and Audience

An important part of prewriting is answering these two questions:

• Why am I writing?
• Whom am I writing for?

The answers to these questions will have a major impact on your writing. Why? Read on to find out.

Why Am I Writing?

When you write, you must have a reason for writing. Common reasons for writing are to entertain, to inform, to persuade, and to express oneself. Each time you write, you need to ask yourself: Why am I writing this?

Of course, your reason for writing might be "Because I have to," but while that *is* a reason, it is not a reason that will help you very much. Knowing your goals for your writing will help you focus your writing.

For example, you are writing an account of a visit to the beach. Do you want to entertain your audience? If so, then you might focus on the amusing things that happened or the interesting people you met. Do you want to inform your audience? If so, then you might focus on facts about the beach. You can have more than one reason for writing. Perhaps you wish to entertain *and* inform your audience about the beach. You might blend amusing incidents with informative facts. Whatever reason you choose, it's important to have one.

You may know your reasons before you begin writing. You may figure them out as you write. As with other parts of your writing, you may revise your reasons as you work.

Whom Am I Writing for?

You answer this question by identifying your audience, the people you are writing for. For a school writing assignment, your audience will probably be your teacher and perhaps your classmates. For a letter, your audience will be whomever the letter is addressed to. For a journal, your audience will be you. In each case, thinking about your audience helps you decide what to say.

Each time you write, ask yourself:

- What does my audience know?
- What might they want to know?
- What do I want to tell them?

The answers to these questions will help you decide what information you want to include or exclude when you write.

Your audience can also influence your level of language. In some situations, you would use more formal language. Imagine writing a letter to the editor of a newspaper or an article for a magazine. In other situations, such as a letter to a relative or a story for a friend, you would use more informal language.

Consider how writing for young children might be different from writing for adults. For young children, you might write about only one main idea with a few details. You would use short sentences, easy words, and very informal language. For adults, you might write about several main ideas with many details. You would use longer, more complex sentences, difficult words, and more formal language.

Drafting

Getting Organized

You have chosen your topic, chosen some details, considered your reasons for writing, and thought about your audience. You have a lot of ideas. Now what? It is time to write your first draft.

Drafting is putting your ideas down on paper. There are many different ways to draft, probably as many ways as there are writers. With practice, you will find out what kind of drafting works best for you.

Some writers like to sketch out a plan before they begin writing. They might make a list of ideas in a particular order or an outline that lists major topics and their subtopics. Then they write a draft following the list or outline. Some writers like to just write down their ideas as the ideas come to them and then rearrange, add, or delete ideas afterward.

A draft is only a first writing. You have to read the draft and decide what to keep and what to change. Then you write a second draft that reflects those changes. You might write several drafts before you have one you consider final. Also, drafting may send you back to prewriting to look for more ideas or details or even to reconsider your topic. Then you would write another draft.

Remember, the purpose of drafting is to get going on the writing. Do not stop to struggle with writing the perfect beginning sentence. That can come later.

Here are some ways to organize your details:

• Details can be organized around a main idea. Write a sentence that tells your main idea and then write all the details (facts, reasons, examples) that support that idea. This kind of organization is often used in persuasive or informative writing.

• Details can be organized in chronological order, or the order in which events happen. Often signal words, such as *first, next, last,* and *finally,* are used to indicate the sequence of events. Chronological order is often used in stories, directions, and science or history reports.

• Details can be organized by order of importance. The writer gives the most important detail first, then the next most important detail, and so on down to the least important detail. This kind of organization may be used in persuasive or informative writing.

• Details can be organized by the way they are arranged in space. The writer begins at one place and then moves on, left to right, top to bottom, room by room, and so on. Details in descriptive writing are often organized in this way.

Different kinds of writing work best with different kinds of organization. Also, more than one kind of organization can be used in one piece of writing.

Try to write your whole draft at one time. Include everything you can think of. You can always make decisions later about what to keep and what to take out. No matter how clumsy and rough you may think your first draft is, remember you must have a draft in order to have something to work with. Also, by writing, you will clarify your thoughts. You will see what you have and what you need to get.

It is a good idea to put a first draft aside before reading it. Time can make some things clearer. Also, you may wish to get others people's comments and ideas about your writing. Ask someone to read one of your drafts. See pages 110–111 for advice on evaluating your own work and having others evaluate it.

Writing Paragraphs

What is a **paragraph**? You may think of a paragraph as a group of sentences, and so it is. But there is more to a paragraph than that. First, the sentences that make up a paragraph must work together to state and develop the same main idea. Second, the sentences in a paragraph must be arranged in an order that makes sense. Third, a paragraph may contain a topic sentence.

What is a **topic sentence**? It states the main idea of the paragraph. Often a topic sentence is at or near the beginning of a paragraph. A paragraph does not *have* to have a topic sentence, but it is not a bad idea to write one for each paragraph whether you use it or not. The topic sentence can help make the main idea of the paragraph clear to you. And that can help you when you are adding or deleting details in the paragraph.

Another way to focus on the main idea of a paragraph is to write down everything you can think of when you are writing the first draft of the paragraph. Then think about the main idea, or the message you are trying to get across. Take out any details that are not related to that main idea. Add details that help develop that main idea.

What makes a good paragraph? In a good paragraph, all the sentences stay focused on the paragraph's main idea. They explain and support the main idea by giving details such as facts, incidents, examples, and reasons. (See pages 100–101 about gathering details to develop a topic.) The sentences also give all the information that readers need to  understand the main idea. Moreover, all the sentences are clearly and logically related to each other. They are arranged in an order that readers will have no trouble following and understanding. Just as bricks should fit together well to make a solid wall, sentences should fit together well to make a good paragraph.

One way to help readers is to use transitions that make links between the details in the sentences. Transitions may indicate time (*first, last, today, yesterday, now, then*); they may indicate an arrangement in space (*above, below, inside, outside*); they may indicate order of importance (*first, second, third*); they may indicate a comparison or contrast (*as, like, both, but, yet, however*). These words act as clues for readers, alerting them to relationships between the ideas.

How can you revise a paragraph to make it better?

• Identify the main idea. If you can't identify it, your readers won't be able to, either. Perhaps you need to add a topic sentence stating the main idea.

• Make sure all the details develop the main idea. Delete any details that are unrelated to the main idea.

• Make sure you have included enough details. Does your paragraph raise more questions than it answers? If so, maybe you need to add more information.

• Make sure the order of the sentences makes sense. Perhaps you need to rearrange the sentences or add some transitions to them.

In a way, writing a good paragraph is a lot like writing a whole story or report. A story or report introduces, develops, and concludes a main idea. Its paragraphs are arranged in a sensible order that readers can easily follow. Its subject is fully and carefully explained. So it is with a good paragraph. A paragraph has a main idea that it introduces (often in a topic sentence), develops (using relevant details), and concludes. The sentences in a paragraph are arranged logically and clearly. And the paragraph contains all the details needed to explain the main idea. So once you know the basics of writing a good paragraph, you know the basics of writing a good story or report.

How to Begin

The introduction to your writing is important. It may be several paragraphs or just one sentence. However long it is, it must tell readers what they will be reading about and it must catch a reader's interest and attention.

It might seem logical to simply announce what you are writing about. For example, "This story is about..." or "My subject is...". For most kinds of writing, such a blunt announcement is just not interesting enough to be a good introduction.

Here are some suggestions for introductions:

• **Begin with a story.** A very short story, or anecdote, especially a humorous one, can be a good way to begin. But remember, the story is intended only to lead to your main topic.

• **Begin with a fact.** You can begin with an interesting or unusual bit of information, something that will immediately attract a reader.

• **Begin with a question.** Asking a question can make a reader read to find the answer. Asking a question addressed to the reader can help involve the reader in the subject right from the start.

• **Begin with a quotation.** Sometimes a piece of writing will begin with a quotation by an expert on the topic or by a famous person.

One of the best ways to improve your own introductions is to pay close attention to the introductions of the stories and articles you read. See what other writers do to try to grab a reader's attention. Then the next time you write, try an introduction like one of those you admired.

How to End

As with the introduction, the conclusion to your writing is important. It may be a paragraph or a single sentence. Whatever its length, the conclusion must tell your reader clearly and strongly "The End," but without actually using those words!

Worse than actually saying "The End" is having no ending at all, just a kind of trailing off that leaves your reader dissatisfied or confused. You may have a terrific introduction and wonderful ideas expressed in solid paragraphs and then ruin the whole thing with a weak conclusion.

In general, the conclusion is your last chance to get across to the reader whatever it is you have been trying to say in the rest of your writing. A conclusion is not the place to introduce anything new; it is the place to look back at what has gone before.

Here are some suggestions for conclusions:

• **End with a summary.** Most nonfiction writing ends with a review or summary of what was presented in the body of the writing. This approach is helpful because it leaves the reader with a clear restatement of the main idea.

• **End with a suggestion.** In persuasive writing, a writer may end by offering a suggestion of something that the reader should think or do. This suggestion is usually related to whatever opinion the writer is expressing in the piece.

• **End with the last event.** Usually, in stories or any kind of writing with a chronological order, whatever happens last in the story or sequence of events is the ending. This happened first, this second, and this last.

As you did with introductions, you should study the conclusions of stories and articles you read to see how other writers end their writing. Which conclusions do you think work and which ones do not? Why? Then, the next time you write, try using one of the conclusions you liked as a guide.

Revising

You have written your first draft. Now what? It is time to revise.

The goal of revising is to improve what you have written. The process of revising involves looking at your work, seeing what you like and do not like, and deciding what you want to change and how you will change it.

Revising may mean doing more than just adding a word here or taking out a word there. You may decide to rearrange paragraphs, reword a section, or add sentences. You may do a little revising; you may do a lot. You may even decide to start over and write a whole new draft!

Like prewriting and drafting, revising can take place at any time. You are revising as you organize the information about your topic. You are revising as you reorganize the information while you are writing a draft. Moreover, revising can take place many times during the course of completing a piece of writing.

After you have completed a draft, set it aside for a while. Then take it out and read it. By letting some time pass, you will be able to see things in your writing more clearly, which will help you revise.

Read your draft aloud. Hearing the words can help you evaluate your writing. Awkward words or sentences will stand out more. Gaps in your reasoning or arguments will show up more.

Ask yourself questions about your draft:

- Does my introduction catch a reader's attention?
- Is my main idea clear?
- Is my main idea supported by enough details?
- Do all the details relate to the main idea?
- Should any of the details be taken out?
- Do I need to add any paragraph breaks?
- Is my material organized clearly and logically?
- Is there anything I can add that will make my writing more interesting?
- Does my conclusion clearly indicate "The End"?

Other people can give you advice about your writing. Read your draft to them, or let them read it. There is no better way to find out whether or not you got your message across clearly than to have another person read your writing.

Encourage your reader to offer specific comments and suggestions. A vague "very nice" comment is not very helpful to you. You need to know what was good (and bad) and why. If necessary, ask your reader questions such as these:

- Did anything in my writing confuse you?
- What did you like best or find most interesting?
- What do you think is my main idea?
- Did I answer any questions you might have about my topic?

Listen carefully to what your reader has to say. Do not take the comments too personally; remember, you asked for the person's advice. And after all, you do not have to follow this advice if you do not want to.

Use both your own evaluation and the comments of others to figure out what works and what does not work in your writing. Then you can revise to eliminate problems.

Proofreading

Once you think you have finished any major revisions to your writing, proofread your work. You show respect for yourself and your reader when you make your writing as readable as possible. Now is the time to look for and correct mistakes in spelling, grammar, punctuation, and capitalization. Such things may seem minor, especially when compared to larger issues such as good organization of ideas, solid topic sentences, and sufficient detail. But mechanical errors can distract and confuse a reader. You want the reader to pay attention to your writing and your ideas, *not* your mistakes.

Here are some strategies you can use when you proofread:

• Proofread slowly and carefully. You might make a checklist of questions. (See the example below.) The questions should reflect any particular areas in which you have had difficulty before.

Spelling
☐ Have I spelled all the words correctly?
(If you keep a list of problem words as suggested on page 118, use the word list as part of your checklist.)

Grammar
☐ Have I written complete sentences?
☐ Have I used the correct verb forms?
☐ Do the subjects and verbs agree?
(See pages 5–70 for information on grammar.)

Capitalization
☐ Have I capitalized the first words of sentences?
☐ Have I capitalized proper nouns?
(See pages 72–78 for information on capitalization.)

Punctuation
☐ Have I used an end mark after every sentence?
☐ Have I used commas correctly?
(See pages 79–94 for information on punctuation.)

• Set your work aside and come back to proofread it later. It will be easier to see your mistakes then.

• Proofread aloud. This can be helpful in checking for complete sentences, end punctuation, and commas in sentences.

• Proofread more than once. Look for different things each time. You might check for grammar errors in one reading, capitalization errors in a second reading, and so on.

• Proofread with a dictionary and a grammar handbook nearby. You can use these sources to check any questions you might have. As you read, mark the places where you have questions, finish reading, and then answer the questions.

• Use a computer spell checker, but do not rely on it alone. A computer spell checker will catch some spelling errors, but it cannot help when you write *there* instead of *their* or *student* when you meant *students.* You must proofread your writing yourself to find those kinds of mistakes.

• Ask someone else to proofread your work. This can be helpful, of course, but it is still best to proofread your own work at least once.

You can help make your proofreading faster and more efficient by using proofreading marks. Put the appropriate mark at the place where you mean to make the change.

Here are some common proofreading marks followed by an example of how to use the marks when proofreading a paragraph.

Proofreading Marks

≡ Capitalize the letter.
/ Make the capital letter lowercase.
⊙ Add a period.
⌄ Add a comma.
∧ Add the letter(s) or word(s).
℮ Take out the letter(s) or word(s).
⌒ Close up the space.
¶ Begin a new paragraph.
∿ Reverse the position of the letters or words.

The English Writer Arthur conan Doyle created the fictoinal

detective Sherlock Holmes. Holmes first appeared in the story "A

Study in Scarlet" in 1887. Tired of writing stor ies about Holmes,

Doyle tried to kill off the charac ter in 1893, but an out raged

public forced him Doyle to bring Holmes back.

Publishing

You probably think of publishing as getting your writing published in a newspaper or magazine or as a book. Think of publishing instead as any way you can present and share your writing with an audience, which includes getting it printed.

The following publishing ideas are suitable for all kinds of writing:

• Produce a classroom newspaper or magazine several times a year or once a month. The newspaper or magazine will feature writing by you and your classmates. Share this newspaper or magazine with students in other classes or with family members at home.

• Submit your writing to the school newspaper or to a local or community newspaper or magazine.

• Get together with others and take turns reading your work aloud. Discuss each other's writing afterward.

• Post your writing on the class bulletin board for all to read.

• Give your writing as an oral presentation.

• Make copies of your writing to share with anyone who is interested, including friends and family members.

Some publishing ideas, such as the following, are more suitable for certain kinds of writing:

• Mail a letter to the person it is intended for.

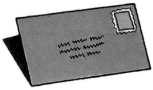

• Make a persuasive essay or opinion piece into a letter to the editor and submit it to a newspaper.

• Make a persuasive essay or opinion piece into a poster and arrange to hang it in the lunchroom or a hallway.

• Use a persuasive essay or opinion piece as part of a debate.

• Submit book, movie, or music reviews to the school newspaper.

• Read a story aloud to younger students or family members.

• Turn a story into a skit or play for younger students or family members.

• Read aloud and perform a demonstration with a report that explains a process.

One part of completing the writing process is finding a way to share your final product with an audience. Thinking about your writing is also part of completing the writing process.

To gain from your writing experience, think about these questions:

• What did you do this time that you would do the same the next time you write?
• What did you do this time that you would do differently?
• Which parts did you like?
• Which parts did you have trouble with?

You might write the answers to these questions. When you save your writing, save the answers to the questions, too. Start a writing portfolio in a notebook or a folder. Keep your writing, your answers, and your writing ideas in your portfolio.

Skills for Writing

Using a Dictionary

A **dictionary** is a special kind of reference book that lists words, their spellings, and their definitions. A dictionary also gives other information about words. Knowing how a dictionary is organized can help you when you need to use this important book.

1. The words listed in a dictionary are called **entry words**. The entry words are listed in alphabetical order, that is, the order of the letters in the alphabet, A to Z.

2. At the top of every page of a dictionary are two words called **guide words.** You can use guide words to find the page that has the word you are looking for. The guide word on the left is the first entry word on a page. The guide word on the right is the last entry word on the page. If your word comes alphabetically between the two guide words on a page, then it will appear on that page.

3. The **dictionary entry** is the information about an entry word. First, the entry word is shown divided into syllables. Next is the **pronunciation guide,** which is the entry word spelled using symbols that stand for sounds. (The **pronunciation key,** found at the bottom of the right-hand pages or at the front of the dictionary, explains the symbols.) Next, the entry gives the word's **part of speech** using an abbreviation such as *n.* or *adj.* This is followed by the **definition**, which tells the meaning of the word. An entry may also include the word's **history**—where it came from and how it developed— and **synonyms** for the word. A synonym is another word with the same or a similar meaning.

Different dictionaries may organize the information in their entries in different ways. Some may include information that others do not. Usually, a dictionary has an introduction that explains how the dictionary is organized.

Spelling Help

Here are some things you can do to help yourself become a better speller:

1. When you first see a new word, look at it closely. Pronounce the word carefully, emphasizing each syllable. Then look at each letter. (Many common spelling errors result from leaving out letters or syllables.) Picture the complete word in your mind. Write the word. Check to see that you have spelled it correctly.

2. Keep a list of problem words. Make a list of any words that you have had trouble spelling, particularly any words that you have misspelled more than once. Use the list as your personal reference source.

3. Use a dictionary. Look up a word whenever you are not absolutely certain of its spelling. (Even if you are certain, it can't hurt to double-check!)

4. Proofread your writing. Careful proofreading can help you find many common errors, including misspelled words.

5. Create **mnemonics,** or memory devices. A mnemonic is anything that helps you remember how a particular word is spelled. For example, the singing rhyme for spelling *Mississippi (M-i-s-s, i-s-s, i-p-p-i, it used to be so hard to spell...)* is a mnemonic. To remember that *necessary* has one *c* and two *s*'s, you might make up a sentence such as *It is necessary to call Susie and Sam.* To remember that *accommodate* has two *c*'s and two *m*'s, you might make a picture in your mind of **two c**ats chasing **two m**ice. Think about creating mnemonics for problem words on your list. Mnemonics are best for the words you have trouble spelling. You might not want to try them for every new word you learn.

6. Remember a few spelling rules.

• Is it *ie* or *ei?* Use *ie* when the letters spell the long *e* sound, except after *c.*

bel**ie**ve	p**ie**ce	f**ie**ld
c**ei**ling	rec**ei**ve	dec**ei**ve

Exceptions to this rule:

seize   leisure
either   neither

• When a prefix is added to a word, the spelling of the word does not change.

un + likely = unlikely   mis + spell = misspell
dis + agree = disagree   re + view = review

• For most words with a final *e*, drop the *e* before adding a suffix that begins with a vowel. Keep the *e* before adding a suffix that begins with a consonant.

write + ing = writing   move + ed = moved
hope + less = hopeless   care + ful = careful

• For words ending in a consonant and a *y*, change the *y* to *i* before adding a suffix that does *not* begin with *i*.

hurry + ed = hurried   pity + ful = pitiful
hurry + ing = hurrying   pity + ing = pitying

• Double the final consonant before adding a suffix that begins with a vowel if

(a) the word has one syllable and ends with one consonant preceded by one vowel.

run + ing = running
hot + est = hottest

(b) the word has more than one syllable, ends with one consonant preceded by one vowel, and is accented on the last syllable.

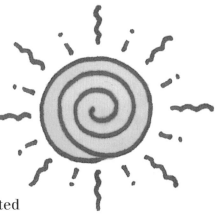

admit + ed = admitted
forget + ing = forgetting
offer + ed = offered
profit + ing = profiting
(*Offer* and *profit* are accented on the first syllable.)

Using a Thesaurus

A **thesaurus** is a special kind of reference book that contains synonyms and antonyms for words. **Synonyms** are words that have the same or similar meanings. *Cold* and *cool* are synonyms because they have similar meanings. **Antonyms** are words that have opposite meanings. *Cold* and *hot* are antonyms because they have opposite meanings.

You can use a thesaurus to make your writing more specific. It can help you find words that have exactly the meaning you want. You can also use a thesaurus to make your writing more interesting or exciting. It can help you find many different words to express the same meaning.

Some thesauruses are arranged alphabetically. If you looked up the word *say* in one of these thesauruses, you might see an entry like this one:

> **say,** *v.* **1.** speak, remark, pronounce, utter, affirm, allege **2.** tell, state, declare, express, argue, word **3.** recite, repeat, reiterate, rehearse **4.** report, allege, maintain, hold

Some thesauruses are arranged with an index at the back. If you looked up the word *say* in one of these thesauruses, you might see a list like this one in the index:

> **say**
> *affirm* 532 vb.
> *speak* 579 vb.

Then if you turned to section 579, you might see a list like this:

> **Vb.** *speak,* mention, say; utter, articulate 577 vb. *voice,* pronounce, declare 524 vb. *hint,* talk 570 vb. *recite,* read, dictate

Any of the words in either entry might be good ones to use in place of *say,* but it is important to remember that synonyms do have slightly different meanings. It is a good idea to check the meaning of a synonym in a dictionary before using it in a sentence.

recite   tell   DECLARE   report

express

Choosing the Right Word

Here are some commonly misused and misspelled words. Writers often have problems with these words because they sound alike or very similar. Use the meanings and example sentences to help you choose the right word to use.

Accept-Except

Accept is a verb meaning "to receive" or "to agree to." *Except* is most often used as a preposition meaning "not including." But *except* can also be used as a verb meaning "to leave out."

I **accept** your invitation to the party.
Everyone **except** Jason will be coming. He will be **excepted** from attending.

Affect-Effect

Affect is most often used as a verb meaning "to influence." It is also sometimes used as a noun meaning "feelings" or "how a person appears to feel." *Effect* is most often used as a noun meaning "result of an action."

The water pollution will **affect** the fish.
The counselor observed the patient's **affect**.
The **effect** of the water pollution is dead fish.

Council-Counsel

Council is a noun meaning "a group of people called together to discuss questions and give advice." *Counsel* as a noun means "advice." *Counsel* as a verb means "to give advice to."

The town **council** discusses land development.
Experts give them **counsel** on different issues.
A professor **counsels** them on animal habitats.

Emigrate–Immigrate

Emigrate means "to go from a country" and settle somewhere else. *Immigrate* means "to come into a country" and settle there.

> In the 1850s, many people **emigrated** from Ireland. Many Irish **immigrated** to the United States.

Its–It's

Its is a possessive pronoun. It has no apostrophe. *It's* is a contraction for *it is*. The apostrophe replaces the missing letter *i*.

> **It's** time to take the dog for a walk.
> The dog carries **its** leash in **its** mouth.

Principal–Principle

Principal as an adjective means "most important." *Principal* as a noun means "head of a school." *Principle* means "general truth" or "rule of conduct."

> Ms. Javier is the **principal** of our school. Her **principal** task is to keep the school running. She believes in the **principle** of fairness.

Their–There–They're

Their is a pronoun meaning "belonging to them." It is the possessive form of *they*. *There* is usually an adverb meaning "in or to that place." *They're* is a contraction for *they are*.

> **Their** car broke down on the way to the airport. They were supposed to be **there** by 5:00 P.M. **They're** going to be late meeting the plane.

To-Too-Two

To is usually a preposition meaning "toward" or "in the direction of." *Too* is an adverb meaning "also" or "very." *Two* is the word for the number 2.

Too many birds came **to** the bird feeder.
A cardinal and a blue jay are waiting, **too.**
There isn't room for **two** more.

Whose-Who's

Whose is the possessive form of the pronoun *who.* It has no apostrophe. *Who's* is a contraction for *who is* or *who has.* The apostrophe replaces the missing letter or letters.

Whose turn is it to pick up the pizza?
Do you know **who's** going to pick up the pizza?

Your-You're

Your is the possessive form of the pronoun *you.* It has no apostrophe. *You're* is a contraction for *you are.* The apostrophe replaces the missing letter *a.*

Your sister is looking for you.
She says **you're** supposed to go home now.

See pages 34–35 for information on using confusing verbs and page 64–65 for information on using confusing prepositions.

Index